COUNCIL SPEECHES

OF

VATICAN II

April 4, 1964

For Beatrice and Ed;
whose marriage
will image the
unity of Christ
and his Church
which is the
concern of
this book.

Father Dan

COUNCIL SPEECHES OF VATICAN II

edited by

Küng
^{Hans}

Congar, O.P.
^{Yves}

O'Hanlon, S.J.
^{Daniel}

AN ORIGINAL DEUS BOOK
Paulist Press (Paulist Fathers)
GLEN ROCK · NEW JERSEY

Library of Congress
Catalog Card Number: 64-18548

Published by the Paulist Press
Editorial Office: 401 W. 59th St., N.Y. 19, N.Y.
Business Office: Glen Rock, New Jersey

Manufactured in the
United States of America

Contents

5

PART II

RENEWAL OF THE CHURCH

PART III

REUNION OF ALL CHRISTIANS

Editors' Preface

The Second Vatican Council—a great symbol of hope for the Catholic Church, for Christianity and for the world! Will it fulfill the hopes it has aroused? Too much still remains uncertain. But great things have already taken place. Evidence of this is the new atmosphere in the Catholic Church and in the whole Christian world, a new atmosphere of openness, of freedom, of willingness to understand, of committed dialogue and of mutual Christian service. Evidence of actual accomplishment is found in what the Council has already done, above all in the great reform of the liturgy which has been definitively accepted. It will open up a new era in the history of Christian worship, and also of personal and ecclesial spirituality. Further evidence of achievement are the important speeches given at the Council, which solidify the gains already made, challenge the contemporary Church to action, and tell of what lies ahead.

There is no better way of sensing the spirit which animates the Second Vatican Council than to read these speeches and meditate on them. Reflection on the Gospel of Christ, serious resolve to reform, ecumenical involvement, honest facing of the problems of our times, sober realism, constructive criticism, suggestions which point ahead

11

—all of this finds a voice in the short talks of the bishops brought together in this volume.

For the editors, finding suitable speeches for this collection was no problem at all. The only problem was that of selection. What were the principles which guided our choice? It was not our intention to include everything. We took as our norm the program for the Council formulated with such clarity and depth by Paul VI. His four points—self-awareness of the Church, renewal, reunion of Christians, dialogue with the world — provided both the exterior and inner structure of our book. The appropriate section of his opening discourse for the second session is placed as a guiding light at the beginning of each section of the book. Only those talks have been included which were given in the spirit of this opening discourse. Those which were expressions of doctrinaire narrowness, petty criticism and unproductive defense of the status quo were by that very fact disqualified.

From the constructive speeches those were chosen which took a stand on a specific problem and possessed a compact unity and completeness. Many talks which were made up of a series of short comments on different points of a schema, were, despite their real excellence, less suited to a collection of this kind. In the speeches which were chosen, direct references to the text of the schemata were omitted, since the text remains *sub secreto* and these direct references were of no importance for our purpose anyway. It goes without saying that none of the speeches have been published without authorization from those who delivered them. We want to thank them for graciously allowing others to profit from the doctrinal contribution they made at the Council. Finally, we were concerned to show in our collection some of the diverse variety of peoples and problems which is so characteristic of this Council.

Council speeches are not fancy oratory. They are plans for action. They are a demanding challenge. Everything depends on whether these words are followed by *actions!* That is what the Catholic Church hopes for, what Christians everywhere hope for. That is the hope of the whole world.

Rome, at the end of the second session of the Council, December, 1963.

> Yves Congar, O.P. (Strasbourg)
> Hans Küng (Tübingen)
> Daniel O'Hanlon, S.J.
>   (Los Gatos, California)

**Dedicated to Pope John
Who Gave His Life
For The Council**

We cannot recall this event without remembering our predecessor of happy and immortal memory whom we greatly loved, John XXIII. To all of us who saw him in this seat, his name brings back the memory of his lovable and priestly image. When he opened the first session of this Second Vatican Council last October 11th, he gave a speech which appeared to be prophetic for our century—not only for the Church, but for the entire society of mankind. That speech still echoes in our memory and conscience while it directs the path the Council must take. It frees us from all doubt and weariness which we may encounter on this difficult journey.

Oh dear and venerated Pope John! May gratitude and praise be rendered to you. Surely under a divine inspiration you convoked this Council to open new horizons for the Church and to channel over the earth the new and yet untapped spring waters of Christ our Lord's doctrine and grace.

You did not act from earthly motives nor from the force of circumstances. But you acted as one who understood the Divine Will, one who penetrated into the dark and tormented needs of our age. You have resumed the interrupted course of the First Vatican Council. You have banished the uneasy assumption wrongly deduced from that Council that the supreme powers conferred on the Roman Pontiff to govern the Church —powers acknowledged by that Council—were sufficient without the help of ecumenical councils.

You have summoned your brothers in the episcopate, the successors of the Apostles, not only to continue the interrupted study and suspended legislation, but to feel united with the Pope in a single body, to be comforted and directed by him "that the sacred deposit of Christian doctrine be guarded and taught more effectively" (*A.A.S.* 1962, p. 790).

But to the principal aim of the Council you added another which is more urgent and at this time more salutary—the pastoral aim—when you declared: "Nor is the primary purpose of our work to discuss one article or another of the fundamental doctrine of the Church," but rather, "to consider how to expound Church teaching in a manner demanded by the times" (*ibid.* 791-792).

You have strengthened the convictions of the teaching authority of the Church regarding Christian doctrine. It is not only truth to be investigated by reason illumined by faith, but it is also the generative word of life and action. You have strengthened our opinion that the authority of the Church ought not to be limited to the condemnation of errors. Rather this authority should be extended to proclaim that positive and vital doctrine which is the source of its fecundity.

The teaching office of the Church, which is neither wholly theoretical nor wholly negative, must in the Council manifest ever more the life-giving power of the message of Christ who said: "The words that I have spoken to you are spirit and life" (John 6:64). Hence we shall ever keep in mind the norms which you, the first Father of this Council, have wisely laid down and which we may profitably repeat here:

"Our task is not merely to guard this precious treasure, namely our Faith, as if we were only concerned with antiquity, but to dedicate ourselves with an earnest will and without fear to that work which our era demands of us, pursuing thus the path which the Church has followed for nearly 20 centuries. Hence, that method of presenting the truth must be used which is more in conformity with a magisterium prevalently pastoral in character" (*A.A.S.* 1962, pp. 791-792).

We shall have due regard for the great question of the unity in one flock of those who believe in Christ and wish to be members of the Church which, you John, have called the paternal home whose doors are open to all. The Council which you have promoted and inaugurated will proceed faithfully along the path you pointed out, so that with God's help may it reach the goal you have so ardently desired and hoped for. Let us therefore go forward, Brothers.

POPE PAUL VI
Opening Address of the Second Session

POPE PAUL VI

Christ the Beginning, Way, and Goal of the Council

From what point, dear brothers, do we set out? If we turn our thoughts to the law of God himself, instead of directing our attention to the practical considerations just mentioned, what is the road we should follow? And what is the goal toward which our journey leads? The journey is made within the framework of human history, bearing all the marks of time, and is conditioned by all the limitations of our present life. Yet at every moment we must be guided by the ultimate and decisive goal which we know awaits us at journey's end.

To these three questions, simple yet altogether essential, we know well that there is only one answer, an answer which should resound within our hearts and be proclaimed to the world around us. The answer is Christ: Christ from whom we begin; Christ who is both the road we

travel and our guide on the way; Christ, our hope
and our final end.

O, may this Council be fully aware of this relationship between ourselves and Jesus Christ,
a relationship which has a hundred different aspects yet is always the same, which stands firm
yet is the source of life and movement, full of
mystery yet limpid in its clarity, a relationship
which demands much from us, yet fills us with
joy. May the Council be deeply conscious of this
relationship between the holy and living Church
—which is really our own selves—and Christ,
from whom we come, by whom we live, and
toward whom we go.

Let there be no other guiding light for this
gathering but Christ, the light of the world. Let
the interest of our minds be turned to no other
truth but the words of the Lord, our one master;
let us be guided by no other desire but to be unconditionally loyal to him. Let the only trust
which sustains us come from those words of his
which shore up our pitiful weakness: "And behold I am with you forever, even to the end of
the world" (Matt. 28:30).

Would that we could at this moment raise to
our Lord Jesus Christ a voice worthy of him!
As the Sacred Liturgy says: "You alone, O Christ,
we know; we seek you with a pure and upright
intention and ask you in our joys and sorrows
to regard the feelings of our heart" (Hymn of
Lauds for Wednesdays).

As we thus invoke him, he seems to present
himself to our rapt gaze with the majesty proper
to the "Pantocrator" (all mighty)—the glorious

Christ of your basilicas—O brothers of the Eastern Churches, as well as those of the West.

In a certain sense we recognize in ourself the
figure of a humble worshiper, our predecessor
Honorius II. He is portrayed adoring Christ
in a beautiful mosaic in the apse of the
Basilica of St. Paul. That Pontiff of short
stature is represented there prostrate, kissing the
feet of a Christ of gigantic dimensions. This
Christ, in the likeness of a royal and majestic
teacher, presides over and blesses the people
gathered in the Basilica — a symbol of the
Church.

Indeed, this picture is reproduced before us—
not on a wall with lines and colors—but in reality.
This reality acknowledges in Christ the source
of redeemed humanity. This reality sees in
Christ the Church. It sees in the Church, Christ's
extension and continuation both earthly and
heavenly. This recalls to our mind the apocalyp-
tic vision of St. John: "He showed me a river of
the water of life, clear as crystal, coming forth
from the throne of God and of the Lamb" (Apoc.
22:1).

It seems to us opportune that this Council
should have as its starting point this vision, or
mystical celebration, which acknowledges him,
our Lord Jesus Christ, to be the Incarnate Word,
the Son of God and the Son of Man, the Redeemer of the world, the Hope of humanity and
its supreme Master, the Good Shepherd, the
Bread of Life, the High Priest and our Victim,
the sole Mediator between God and men, the
Savior of the world, the eternal King of ages;

and which declares that we are his chosen ones, his disciples, his apostles, his witnesses, his ministers, his representatives and his living members together with the whole company of the faithful, united in this immense and unique Mystical Body, his Church, which he is forming by means of faith and the sacraments, as generations of mankind succeed one another—a Church which is spiritual and visible, fraternal and hierarchical, temporal today and eternal tomorrow.

Venerable Brethren, recall these facts of the greatest importance. Christ is our Founder and Head. He is invisible, yet real. We receive everything from him and constitute with him the whole Christ—this whole Christ we find expressed in the writings of St. Augustine and in the entire doctrine of the Church. If we recall this, we shall be better able to understand the main objectives of this Council.

For reasons of brevity and better understanding we enumerate here those objectives in *four points*:

1. The self-awareness of the Church,
2. Its renewal,
3. The bringing together of all Christians in unity,
4. The dialogue of the Church with the contemporary world.

PART I
Self-Awareness
of the Church

POPE PAUL VI
Bishop of Rome

1

The Task

There can be no doubt whatever of the Church's desire and need and duty to give a more thorough definition of herself. We are all familiar with the magnificent images with which Holy Scripture describes the nature of the Church: the building raised up by Christ, the house of God, the temple and tabernacle of God, his people, his flock, his vine, his field, his city, the pillar of truth, and finally, the bride of Christ, his Mystical Body.

In meditating on these revealing images, the Church has come to see herself as an historic, visible and hierarchically organized society, animated by a mysterious principle of life. The celebrated encyclical of Pope Pius XII, *Mystici Corporis,* has in part answered the Church's longing to express her nature in a full doctrinal form, but has also served to spur her to give herself a more exhaustive definition.

The First Vatican Council treated of the subject and many external influences have caused it to receive attention from learned men both within the Church and without. Among these influences are the intensification of social life in temporal matters, the development of communications, the need to judge the various Christian denominations according to the true and univocal conception found in divine Revelation.

Almost twenty centuries after the foundation of Christ's religion, the Catholic Church and other religious communities bearing the glorious name of Christian Churches have everywhere undergone great expansion. Yet it should not be surprising that the concept of the Church which Christ founded and the Apostles expanded still needs to be expressed with greater precision. Its full and profound truth still needs to be more and more brought to light. For the Church is a mystery. It is a reality imbued with the hidden presence of God. It lies, then, within the very nature of the Church to be always open to new and greater exploration.

Human thought moves forward. Man advances from empirically observed fact to scientific truth; from one truth he derives another by logical deduction, and, confronted by the complexity and permanence of reality, he bends his mind now to one of its aspects, now to another. It is thus that thought evolves. The course of its evolution can be traced in history.

It moreover seems to us that the time has now come to more and more examine, coordinate and explore the truth about the Church of Christ. Perhaps the expression should not take the form of a solemn dogmatic definition. Rather the Church should declare by a more serious and clear magisterium what she considers herself to be.

This self-awareness of the Church is clarified by faithful adherence to the words and thought of

Christ, by respectful attention to the teaching of ecclesiastical tradition and by docility to the interior illumination of the Holy Spirit, who seems to be requiring of the Church today that she should do all she can to make known what she really is.

We consider it a good sign that the Spirit of Truth in this Council has greatly illumined the teaching authority of the Church and proposes a clearer doctrine of the nature of the Church. As a result, the Church—as bride of Christ—might seek her image in him; and in him, moved by burning love, she may strive to reveal her true form: the beauty which he himself wishes to shine within his Church.

For this reason, the principal concern of this session of the Council will be to examine the intimate nature of the Church. It will be to express in human language—as far as possible—a definition which will explain the true and primary structure of the Church and clarify its multiple and salvific mission. This theological doctrine can receive many noteworthy developments which even may be carefully considered by our separated brothers. We ardently hope that this doctrine will make easier the path toward common agreement.

Among the various and diverse questions to be treated by the Council, the first pertains to you as bishops of the Church of God. Taking for granted the dogmatic declarations of Vatican I concerning the Roman Pontiff, we confidently and expectantly look forward to this discussion which shall develop the doctrine of the episcopate, its function and its relationship with Peter.

For us personally, it will provide doctrinal and practical standards by which our apostolic office, endowed though it is by Christ with the fullness and sufficiency of power, may receive more help and support, in ways to be determined, from a more effective and responsible collaboration with our beloved and venerable brothers in the episcopate.

Next it will be necessary to elucidate the teaching regarding the different components of the visible and mystical body, the pilgrim, militant Church on earth, that is, priests, religious, the faithful, and also the separated brethren who are called to adhere to it more fully and completely.

The importance of this doctrinal aspect of the Council's work will be obvious to all. From it the Church can draw an illuminating, uplifting and sanctifying self-knowledge. May God fulfill our hopes!

CARDINAL LEON SUENENS

Archbishop of Mechlin-Brussels,
Belgium

2

The Charismatic Dimension of the Church

The remarks made about the charisms of the Christian people are so few that one could get the impression that charisms are nothing more than a peripheral and unessential phenomenon in the life of the Church. Now the vital importance of these charisms for building up the Mystical Body must be presented with greater clarity and consequently at greater length. What is to be completely avoided is the appearance that the hierarchical structure of the Church appear as an administrative apparatus with no intimate connection with the charismatic gifts of the Holy Spirit which are spread throughout the life of the Church.

The time of the Church, which is on pilgrimage through the centuries until the parousia of the Lord, is the time of the *Holy Spirit*. For it is through the Holy Spirit that the glorified Christ unifies the eschatological people of God, purifies them, fills them with life and leads them to all truth, and this in spite of the weaknesses and sins of this people. The Holy Spirit is thus the first fruits (Rom. 8:23), the first installment of the Church (2 Cor. 1:22; 5:5), in this world. Therefore the Church is called the dwelling of God in the Spirit (Eph. 2:22).

It follows from this that the Holy Spirit is not given to pastors only but to each and every Christian. "Do you not know that you are the temple of God, and that the Holy Spirit dwells within you?" says St. Paul to the Corinthians (1 Cor. 3:16).

In baptism, the sacrament of faith, all Christians receive the Holy Spirit. All Christians, "living stones," as they are called, are to be built into a "spiritual dwelling" *oikos pneumatikos* (2 Pet. 2:5). Therefore the whole Church is essentially a truly "pneumatic" or spiritual reality, built on the foundation not only of the Apostles, but—as Ephesus 2:20 says — also of prophets. In the Church of the New Testament God "gave some to be apostles, some prophets, some pastors and teachers" (Eph. 4:11; *see* 3:5).

The Holy Spirit shows himself in the Church in the great number and richness of his spiritual gifts, gifts which Scripture calls *pneumatika* (1 Cor. 12:1; 14:1) or charisms (Rom. 12:6; 1 Cor. 12: 4, 9, 28, 30f; 1 Tim. 4:14; 2 Tim. 1:6; 1 Pet. 4:10). Certainly in the time of St. Paul even very extraordinary and marvelous charisms such as "ecstatic utterance" (1 Cor. 12:10, 28, 30; 14:18, 26; Acts. 19:6) or charisms of healings (1 Cor. 12:9, 28, 30; *see* 1 Cor. 12:10, 12, 28f; Gal.

3:5), were shown forth in the Church. But we should not think that the charisms of the Spirit consist exclusively or even principally in these phenomena which are more extraordinary and marvelous. St. Paul speaks, for example, of the charism of wise speech and knowledge (1 Cor. 12:8), of the charism of faith (1 Cor. 12:9), of the charism of teaching (Rom. 12:7; 1 Cor. 12:28f, 14, 26), of stirring or comforting speech (Rom. 12:8), and administration (Rom. 12:7), of the charism of distinguishing true spirits from false (1 Cor. 12:10), of the charism of helping others and guiding them (1 Cor. 12:28) and so on.

Thus to St. Paul the Church of the living Christ does not appear as some kind of administrative organization, but as a living web of gifts, of charisms, of ministries. The Spirit is given to every individual Christian, the Spirit who gives his gifts, his charisms to each and every one "different as they are allotted to us by God's grace" (Rom. 12:6). "In each of us the Spirit is manifested in one particular way, for some useful purpose" (1 Cor. 12:7) for example "to build up the Church" (1 Cor. 14:12). Each and every Christian, whether lettered or unlettered, has his charism in his daily life, but—as St. Paul says—"All of these must aim at one thing; to build up the Church" (1 Cor. 14:26, *see* 14:3-5).

Listen again to the Apostle who says "Within the Church God has appointed, in the first place apostles, in the second place prophets, thirdly teachers. . . . Are all apostles? all prophets? all teachers?" (1 Cor. 12:28f).

A statement about the Church, then, which would speak only of the Apostles and their successors and fail to speak also about prophets and teachers would be defective in a matter of the highest importance.

What would our Church be without the charism of teachers or theologians? And what would our Church be like without the charism of prophets, that is, men speaking under the inspiration of the Holy Spirit, who speaking out insistently "on all occasions, convenient and inconvenient" woke up the Church at times when she was asleep, to prevent the practice of the Gospel of Christ from being neglected?

It was not in past ages alone, not only in the time of St. Thomas Aquinas or St. Francis of Assisi that the Church was in need of the charisms of teachers and prophets and other ministries; she needs them today as well and needs them in her ordinary everyday life.

So let us pass over the more outstanding charisms and come to the more commonplace charisms. Do we not all know laymen and laywomen in each of our own dioceses who we might say are in a way called by the Lord and endowed with various charisms of the Spirit? Whether in catechetical work, in spreading the Gospel, in every area of Catholic activity in social and charitable works? Do we not know and see in our daily experience that the action of the Holy Spirit has not died out in the Church?

Charisms in the Church without the ministry of pastors would certainly be disorderly, but vice versa, ecclesiastical ministry without charisms would be poor and sterile.

It is the duty of pastors, both those in charge of local and individual Churches and those in charge of the universal Church, through a kind of spiritual instinct to discover the charisms of the Spirit in the Church, to foster them and to help them grow.

It is the duty of pastors to listen carefully and with an open heart to laymen, and repeatedly to engage in a living dialogue with them. For each and every layman has been given his own gifts and charisms, and more often than not has greater experience than the clergy in daily life in the world.

Finally, it is the duty of pastors themselves to aim at the higher charisms (1 Cor. 12:31). It is clear that all the faithful, even those endowed with the greatest gifts, give reverence and obedience to their pastors. But it is also true from the other side that similar attention and reverence is due to those charisms and impulses of the Holy Spirit, who very frequently breathes through Christian laymen who have no position of authority. Consequently St. Paul warns all Christians, pastors included "Do not quench the Spirit, and do not despise prophetic utterances, but bring them all to the test and then keep what is good" (1 Thess. 5: 19-21). This complex of gifts, charisms and ministries can be brought into play and serve to build up the Church only through that freedom of the sons of God which, following St. Paul's example, all pastors must protect and foster.

The suggestions to be made on the level of *doc-*

trine are that the chapter on the people of God be improved in the following ways:

1. Along with the structure of ministry, the charismatic dimension of the Church should be developed in the whole chapter.

2. The importance of charisms in the people of God should be given positive emphasis by more extended and concrete treatment.

3. In particular the importance of prophets and teachers in the Church should be given attention.

4. The relation of pastors to charisms of the faithful should be described in more positive and constructive terms.

5. The teaching of St. Paul about the freedom of the sons of God in the Church should not be forgotten.

On the *practical* level, I suggest that in order to manifest also in the Council itself and before all men, our faith in the charisms given by the Holy Spirit to all believing Christians:

1. The *number* and *range* of lay auditors should be increased.

2. *Women* too should be *invited* as auditors; unless I am mistaken, they make up half of the human race.

3. Finally, religious Brothers and Sisters should be invited, since they too belong to the people of God, have received the Holy Spirit and serve the Church as a choice segment of the Lord's flock.

EDWARD SCHICK

Auxiliary Bishop of Fulda,
Germany

3

Importance of the Local Church

It seems to me that a fuller and more profound exposition is needed of what is said about priests and local Churches, to prevent the suspicion that we do not properly appreciate the importance of the local Church and the priesthood, something at the same time full of difficulties, yet of decisive importance in the care of souls.

The desire which we all share, to show for the episcopacy and the diocese both on the doctrinal and practical level the high regard which they deserve, should not lead us to neglect or undervalue the local Church and the priesthood.

Is it not true that many of those responsibilities, particularly those of teaching, sanctifying and ruling, tasks which could be and actually were performed by the bishops themselves in the Church of the patristic period, are carried on for the faithful in our day not by the bishops themselves but by priests? Is it not priests who do most of the preaching of the Gospel, preside at the Eucharist, administer the sacraments, and provide pastoral care for individuals?

Therefore it is desirable that the specific role, responsibility and dignity of the order of priests be given much more positive emphasis.

This consideration of the order of the priesthood leads us by its very nature to something of the highest importance, namely the local Church or parish, seen not from the point of view of administration, but of theology. Frequently we start from that universal Church which is considered in the New Testament principally in the Captivity Epistles. But we neglect that concept of the equally primitive term *"ekklesia"* which is the Church as a community of Christian believers of a certain city or place. In his great epistles when St. Paul uses the word "Church," he uses this word not so much for the universal Church or for the Church which consists of a nation or diocese, but rather — and primarily — for the Christian community of some city: the Church of the Thessalonians (1 and 2 Thess.), "the Church of God which is at Corinth" (1 Cor. 1:2; 2 Cor. 1:1), indeed even for a community of Christians which is gathered together in some home to celebrate the Eucharist (Rom. 26:5; 1 Cor. 11:18, etc.). The image of the body of Christ in the classic text of 1 Corinthians 12 is applied primarily to the Christian community in the city of Corinth.

So a parish in the theological sense or the community of Christian believers of a certain place, which regularly comes together to celebrate the Eucharist, is itself according to the New Testament "the Church". It is not only a certain administrative "division" of the Church, but is a true representation and manifestation of the universal Church. Furthermore, in this representation not only a part but the whole Christ lives and gives life as Lord of the Church, and performs that mystery which is so great that not even the total and universal Church has anything greater. The local Church in the strictest sense, in other words, the local community, brought together in unity by the Word of God and the Body of Christ, and the universal Church, are two essential poles of one and the same Church.

Our statement would lack a fundamental aspect if it did not consider the Church in the full sense, that is, the universal Church represented by local Churches. We need this ecclesiological foundation in order to properly weigh the theological importance of the parish and its liturgy as the liturgy of the Church.

What is needed, then, can be easily summed up as follows: This Church of God and of Christ truly exists in the local Church, which the Apostle rightly calls Church and to which he even applies the image of the body of Christ. In such Churches God gathers together the faithful through the Gospel of Christ. In each of them the mystery of the Lord's Supper is celebrated, something so great that the whole universal Church can perform nothing greater. It is a mystery by which the complete Christ, present everywhere among his own in each community, manifests himself as the symbol of that unity and love in which he wanted all to be joined together among themselves. In these communities, even though they be small and poor, the whole Christ is present through the one Spirit by whom all are filled with life and united among themselves. He is the Spirit of love, of consolation and of hope, who gives his charisms to each individual, so that they make one body with those varied gifts and bear witness before the world to the hope they have by their calling. Therefore, although local Churches do not make up the universal Church by the mere fact of being externally gathered together, at the same time they are not mere administrative divisions of the Church. We must rather say that each local Church is a true representation of the total and universal Church, which itself carries on its own life in these local Churches.

EMILE JOSEPH DE SMEDT

Bishop of Bruges,
Belgium

4

The Priesthood of All Believers

Jesus Christ is the supreme and eternal high priest. He himself received a triple office from the Father: the priestly office or the office of making holy, the prophetic office or the office of teaching, the kingly office or the office of ruling.

Jesus Christ actually lives here and now in the layman by baptism and strives to make him share actively in his roles of priest, prophet and king. Therefore:

1. *The layman is called to live in union with Christ exercising his priestly office.*

Jesus Christ wishes to accomplish spiritual worship in the layman so that the Father may be glorified and atonement made for sin. The layman, who by his baptism and confirmation in Christ the Priest is a consecrated person, should offer himself with him and in him and through him.

The observance of a kind of external legalism

39

is not enough, but the inner life of the layman must be religious, directed to God. It is with Christ that the layman must pray, generously accomplish his daily work, and bear with patience the contradictions of life to make reparation for the sins of the human family, so that he may offer his very self to him, a living sacrifice, dedicated and fit for his acceptance, a worship offered by mind and heart (Rom. 12:1). This union of the layman with Christ the Priest reaches its peak when he shares in his eucharistic sacrifice.

2. *The layman is called to live in union with Christ exercising his role as prophet.*

The layman in Christ should offer to the Father his daily effort to bear witness to the truth. The layman, enlightened by the Spirit of Christ, and joined personally to others, must be the light of the world.

In the midst of the life of the world the layman must think of his intelligence, will, senses, and body and tools of work as things made sacred by their purpose, given to him by Christ himself. In his family, among those with whom he lives, where he works and plays, in the business world, he must make use of all these gifts to show how a true Christian actually lives his life in practice. The teaching of Christ is not a theory but a rule of life which is to penetrate the whole of practical daily life. In our day, through the layman, Christ the Prophet wishes to show in a kind of empirical and verifiable way just what the Gospel is, as he himself living among men in Palestine once *gave us an example* so that we might go and do likewise.

But in addition to this, Christ the Prophet

preached his teaching by the word. In our day, through the layman, he wants to proclaim the moral values and truths of the faith to the human family. The layman, then, well instructed in the teaching of Christ and animated with a living faith, must with Jesus humbly, trustfully and boldly proclaim the word of God in his family and in social life, so that the word of God may have a swift and glorious course (1 Thess. 3:1) and the Christian solution of its problems may be made known to modern society.

The layman begins by hearing Catholic teaching from the Apostles and their successors. But in the understanding of this teaching which follows, he himself, through the supernatural instinct of faith, has an active part, directed by the teaching authority of the Church—as an instrument of Christ the Prophet, through whose assistance the Church is guarded against betraying the truth—given a deeper understanding of it, and enabled to apply it more faithfully in daily life.

3. *The layman is called to live in union with Christ exercising his role as king.*

Christ did not merely preach the truth to the human intelligence, but he began to renew all things in himself. What was the kingly role of Jesus when he lived on earth? Not a life of glory, but a laborious struggle step by step in conformity with the will of the Creator and heavenly Father to put order into everyday human life on both the natural and supernatural level, and to saturate this life with love. By his earthly life in this world Christ began a new order of things and earned for men a new power.

For with the help of Christ, mankind was given the power through human realities and labor to reach a supernatural goal and a share in that glory which he as the first-born began through his resurrection and ascension. In our day by the layman's help, Christ plans step by step to complete this consecration of the world.

We ask the layman, therefore, to spread the kingdom of peace first of all *in himself,* little by little putting on the new man of God's creating, which shows itself in the just and devout life called for by the truth (Eph. 4: 23-24). In this way the soul, body and all material things which each Christian layman uses in accordance with the order of nature, will be directed to the glory of God and the good of human society.

But Christ wishes more. Through the layman he wants to gradually extend his peaceful rule to the *whole world order.* By his humble service in society the Christian layman must work together with all men of good will so that by education and laws harmony may be restored in the family, in the social order, in the state, in international life. The goal, in brief, is a fully Christian order. Through the layman, Christ wants to make use of technical and scientific progress so that the whole human family may live in a more genuinely human fashion, may have wider access to the benefits of culture, may more fully reach that true peace, happiness and freedom of the sons of God, waiting expectantly for the joy they hope for and the coming of the Lord. In this way the redemption of Christ truly "takes on flesh" in earthly realities. All things are then gradually consecrated, and everything is renewed and taken up under a new head under the peaceful rule of Christ (Eph. 1:10).

This is the sublime vocation of the layman who shares in the priesthood of Christ.

But what are the relations which Christ set up between this universal priesthood and the ministerial priesthood which he entrusted to the pastors of his Church?

To enable the layman to fulfill his priestly, prophetic and kingly office, Jesus Christ gave them the right to be supported, taught and ruled by the offices of the sacred hierarchy.

The High Priest himself works in the *priestly ministry* of the hierarchy so that the layman may have access to the eucharistic sacrifice of our redemption and to the sacraments and the graces which flow from them.

Through the *prophetic ministry* entrusted to the hierarchy, Jesus Christ opens to the layman a sure path to an authentic knowledge and a deeper investigation of the truth of the Gospel.

Through the *kingly ministry* of the sacred hierarchy, Jesus Christ does not leave laymen orphans in their extremely difficult task of renewing all things in Christ, but departs and returns to give them courage so that their hearts may rejoice and no one may take their joy away from them.

STEPHEN LASZLO

Bishop of Eisenstadt,
Austria

5

Sin in the
Holy Church of God

Warnings have often been expressed already in this Council against a neglect of the teaching on the eschatological goal of the Church. The Church cannot be understood except as the eschatological people of God, on pilgrimage through time, proclaiming the death and resurrection of the Lord until he comes (*see* 1 Cor. 11:26). But this eschatological pilgrimage is often understood too abstractly. We might hear talk, for instance, of the difficulties and obscurities of the Church's journey in this world. But if we speak of the pilgrim Church in the biblical sense we understand more than that: we say the Church is on pilgrimage because in all its difficulties and miseries this people is not without fault, not without sin.

The people of God of the New Testament is in this respect the successor of the people of the Old Testament. Often this people wishes to follow the way of the Lord, but strays from it, unfortunately, over and over again; it wants to be faithful,

44

but again and again it is found wanting in fidelity; it wants to live in holiness and justice under the grace of God, but over and over turns out to be sinful and exposed to God's anger. Men of this world often point out that the concrete Church is very different from the Church described by theologians and preachers. Theology seems to describe the Church of *saints,* but life itself seems to show us a Church of *sinners.* What are we to say to this question which is very frequently asked by Christians in our day?

If our answer wants to convince men of our day, it must not be compounded of triumphalism and pretense, but must be realistic and completely sincere. In other words, on this earth we may not proclaim only an ecclesiology of glory; that belongs to the end of time. When we speak of the pilgrim Church, we must always begin from an ecclesiology of the Cross. What does this mean?

We believe in and confess a Church that is holy. But this holiness is not the perfect holiness of God, who, as we pray, "alone is holy". The holiness of the Church is constantly exposed to danger and temptation. It is to Christ alone and not to the Church that these words apply: "because of his likeness to us, he has been tested every way, only without sin" (Heb. 4:15). But when we speak of the Church we must say, "Let us therefore boldly approach the throne of our gracious God, where we may receive mercy and in his grace find timely help" (Heb. 4:16). The Church is always in fresh need of God's mercy, grace, and remission of sins. It wants to be and should be and according to the

will of Christ is the communion of saints, but in
actual fact in this present state on the way to God
it always turns out by the malice of men to be
also a communion of sinners and consequently a
communion of penitents. Thus those sins which
occur in the Holy Church can be removed only by
remission through the grace of God. The Church
is in the world but it is also true that the world is
in the Church, and the arena of this struggle between grace and sin is the heart of man. "We
want one thing because we are in Christ, and we
want something different because we are still in
this world," says St. Augustine (*Commentary on
St. John* 81, 4; PL 35, 1842). It is the very holiness itself of the Church which urges her always
to be a penitent Church, so that she may always
humbly implore afresh from God the remission
of sins.

This takes place daily in the liturgy of the Eucharist, which begins with the "Confiteor" of every
one of the participants without exception. This
also takes place daily in the Lord's prayer, when
the Church prays "forgive us our trespasses". As
early as the sixteenth Council of Carthage (418)
we have an unambiguously clear declaration, excluding all Novatian or Donatist ecclesiology,
which is equivalently a triumphalist and idealist
ecclesiology. The Council says that the *saints*
themselves in the Church must acknowledge that
they are sinners and must always pray, in truth
and not merely out of "humility": "forgive us our
trespasses" (*See* Denz. 106-108).

From this it follows that if we speak of "the
Church without stain or wrinkle" (Eph. 5:27),

this can be understood in the full and strict sense only of the Church in its final and perfect state. As St. Augustine says: "Whenever in these books I have mentioned the Church having no stain or wrinkle, this is not to be understood in the sense that she already is such but rather she is being *prepared* so that she may be such when she will appear in her glorious state. For at present, because of certain ignorance and weakness in her members, the *whole* Church has reason to say every day 'forgive us our trespasses' " (*Retr.* II, 18; PL 32, 637f). The same doctrine is taught by St. Thomas in his *Summa Theologica* (III, q.8, a.3, ad.2). Likewise in the liturgy of the fifteenth Sunday after Pentecost we pray: "May your Church be constantly cleansed and protected by your unfailing mercy, Lord, and since she cannot stand firm without you, may she always be ruled by your grace."

From all of this it follows that our teaching in this matter is to be accurately interpreted, especially on the following four points:

1. We should not be silent about sin in the holy Church of God and even in its hierarchy; furthermore, in similar fashion, we should speak of the glory *and* the sins of the people of God.

2. There should not be only an insistence everywhere on the union of the Church with Christ, but also on the distance of the pilgrim and penitent Church from Christ, who is the Lord of the Church and who alone is holy.

3. It should be explicitly stated that the Church must always be undergoing reform, as the Supreme Pontiff said in his allocution of September

22nd of this year, "that continual reform of which the Church herself, as a human and earthly institution, is constantly in need."

4. Finally, in accordance with the ideas expressed by the Supreme Pontiff in his opening address of the second session of the Council, there should be an explicit confession of the joint responsibility and guilt of our Church for the division of Christians.

ELIAS ZOGHBY

Greek-Melchite Patriarchal
Vicar in Egypt

6

Eastern and Western Tradition in the One Church

If after ten centuries of schism and of separate development the Latin and Eastern Churches still find that they are substantially alike, may we suppose that a thousand years ago they had reasons of great importance for separating? Certainly not! The schism would not have taken place if the Churches of the West and the East were not indirectly involved in the conflict which set the two empires in opposition to one another. There are, in fact, times unfavorable to dialogue and times which are favorable. The Eastern Schism, for which a more ecumenical name might be the Great Christian Schism (for the responsibility is shared by both sides), took place at a time when the Christian East and West could not enter into a productive dialogue on a basis of equality.

The small clashes between the Latin and Eastern Churches, which up to this time had been regarded as trifling incidents between brothers of the same family, took on more and more the disturbing proportions of the great conflict which set the two empires at loggerheads. The Latin Church began to see in this development a resistance to the primatial authority of Peter, and the Orthodox saw in it an attempt to dominate which accorded ill with a primacy of service.

The primacy of the Bishop of Rome, which the tradition of a thousand years had consecrated as the bond of unity, began to be thought of in the East as the extension of one local Church to the Church universal. This was the start of the crisis which ended with the separation.

Some modern Catholic historians, men of outstanding merit, interpret the Great Schism as the checkmate of efforts aimed at applying Roman centralization to the Churches of the East, which during ten centuries of union with Rome had become accustomed to combining unity with legitimate diversity.

The Churches of the East, in fact, opposed centralization from the very beginning and opposed it root and branch. Why? Some say out of loyalty to the civil power. Possibly, others say, out of pride. This has not been proved. The Orientals think differently; the Eastern Churches had practiced a system of collegial synods in Church government during ten centuries of union with the Holy See of Rome, without Rome having found anything abnormal in this system. Furthermore, the Church authorities of the East found no religious justification for the new change in the authentic tradition shared by East and West. Then too, the Eastern Churches, founded by the Apostles and their immediate successors and not owing their birth nor development to the Church of the West, found that they possessed a religious, theological, liturgical, monastic and disciplinary heritage which was different from that of the West, yet not opposed to it. Now it is evident that it does not take long for a Church governed by groups which are strangers to its own tradition to find its own tradition substantially diminished.

So it was understandable that Roman centralization seemed to the Easterners to be a means of imposing uniformity, a development which could cast doubt on the legitimacy of their own religious heritage. Yet this was a religious heritage which they had received from their forefathers through an apostolic succession whose credentials were impeccable.

What was needed then, was a dialogue to make clear, as we are doing today at the Council, the nature of the mystery of the Church, the relation between the primacy and collegiality, between the local diocese of Rome and the primatial power of the Bishop of Rome. But this dialogue could not mature either in the eleventh century or at Florence, because the unfavorable social and political framework of the time made it impossible.

One might ask why God did not intervene to prevent this unfortunate break as he intervenes to prevent all doctrinal error in the Church. The answer is not difficult. In the first place, Christian unity should not be exclusively the work of God, but the work of men as well. But it is also true that since the purpose of the primacy of Peter is to protect the integrity of the Christian heritage, God could not want this same primacy to be exercised in such a way that this integrity would suffer harm. The two authentic and apostolic traditions, complementary but different, *i.e.*, the Latin tradition and the Eastern, are in fact the two halves of the Christian heritage, and taken together make up that total and integral Christianity which, as a whole, inherits the promise of divine protection to the end of time. Any unity which would be made in such a way that either of the apostolic traditions suffered harm would impoverish the Church instead of enriching her.

The Catholic unity toward which ecumenism is moving will be much more comprehensive and fruitful than the ecumenism of the present. The Catholic unity we know today manifests itself as something partial and more Latin than anything else. It groups together the Latin Churches of the West and the Latin Churches founded by them in mission countries, along with the modest little communities of uniate Eastern Churches which in general are substantially Latinized even though they have kept their external liturgical rites. Today only Orthodoxy possesses the authentic Eastern tradition, though at times in a diminished form; only the union of Latin and Orthodox on a level of equality can bring together the apostolic tradition in its fullness and make Catholic unity complete.

I speak of union on a level of equality because on the day that union will be achieved, Orthodoxy will have at least as much to give as to receive. It must, therefore, share in the government of the reunited Church on a level of equality with the Latin Church, under the primacy of Peter, of course. The dialogue between equals which was decided on at the Conference of Rhodes should be undertaken by the Catholic Church with the conviction that she will have as much to gain as Orthodoxy.

Actually the schism has mutilated both Churches. The Western Church, when it lost communion with the Apostolic Sees of the East, lost the most collegial segment of the episcopal college. Centralization was carried out at an extraordinary pace without anyone being able to hold it in check. The Western Church has been governed by the Consistory, by those parts of the Consistory which are the Roman Congregations, and finally, for all practical purposes, by the *Congresso* or weekly meeting of the officials of the Curia.

The Eastern Churches, for their part, have lost, through the Great Schism, communion with the center of unity of the whole Church which is the Bishop of Rome. Excessive decentralization has weakened them considerably, making difficult the regular practice of episcopal collegiality, which nevertheless remains their principal system of government.

But God who draws good from evil, wanted this unhappy break to protect the Orthodox Churches from centralization and Latinization, thus rendering ecumenical dialogue immensely profitable and giving promise of great enrichment for the Church when it is again made one.

This dialogue on an equal basis between Latins

and Orthodox, which was practically impossible at the time of the Great Schism, has today become possible, indeed obligatory, within the human family which is moving more and more toward unity through international bodies where all peoples are equally represented.

This dialogue should be accompanied by an effort at decentralization in the Catholic Church, an effort which the Council has already begun, and in the Orthodox Churches, by an effort of qualified centralization around the successor of Peter and in the framework of traditional collegiality.

In this dialogue, which primarily concerns the Latin and Orthodox Churches, the Eastern Uniates will have a role as witnesses which, though secondary, is nevertheless necessary. In de-Latinizing themselves, they must come at last to live more fully in accordance with traditional Eastern forms, within Catholicism, in order to make Latin Catholics more familiar with these forms and make the dialogue easier and more effective. Indeed, for them this is the only way they can be of some use to the Church of Jesus Christ.

PAUL RUSCH

Bishop of Innsbruck,
Austria

7

Collegiality in the New Testament

These remarks are made in the name of the bishops of Germany and Austria and will deal with the question of the college of bishops. Our opinion on this issue is similar to that of Cardinal Alfrink. The statement and proof of collegiality calls for two stages. First of all: Christ the Lord founded a College of Apostles; secondly, in the early Church the episcopacy is seen to be a college —in other words, collegiality is one of those things which pass on to successive generations.

The first point, then: Christ the Lord established a college. There are three parts to the proof.

(1) Christ *founded* the Apostles as a *college*. For we read in St. Luke 6: 13-16: "When day broke he called his disciples to him, and from among them he chose twelve and named them Apostles: Simon, to whom he gave the name of Peter, and Andrew his brother" and so on to the number of twelve. These names, as the group of the twelve, recur in Matthew 10:1-4 and in Mark

3:13-19. In John the individual names are not listed, but the famous expression "the Twelve" occurs (John 6:70), a name which shows that there was a college. From these texts it is clear that Christ the Lord founded a college of the twelve.

(2) Christ the Lord *gave* special *powers to this college.* In Matthew 18:18 Christ says: "I tell you this: whatever you forbid on earth shall be forbidden in heaven, and whatever you allow on earth shall be allowed in heaven." See also John 20:23: "If you forgive any man's sins, they stand forgiven; if you pronounce them unforgiven, unforgiven they remain."

These declarations are given even more force from the famous text in Matthew 28:19-20: "Go forth therefore and make all nations my disciples; baptize men . . . and teach them to observe all that I have commanded you." From these words it is quite evident that Christ gave special powers to this college, powers, indeed, in which the right of directing the Church is clearly contained. But not each individual can exercise the right of directing the whole Church, as is certain from the text dealing with the primacy, therefore the college of the Twelve as a college has this right.

(3) This *college* also *directed the Church in actual fact.* We read in Acts 6:2: "So the Twelve called the whole body of disciples together and said, 'It would be a grave mistake for us to neglect the word of God in order to wait at table . . .'" And in 6:6 the account continues, "these they presented to the apostles who prayed and laid their hands on them." These words describe the

foundation of the diaconate, which was done by the college.

Again we read in Acts 8:14-15: "The Apostles in Jerusalem now heard that Samaria had accepted the word of God. They sent off Peter and John, who went down there and prayed for the converts, asking that they might receive the Holy Spirit." We might be surprised that the text says: "They sent off Peter." Yet this is not at all surprising, since Peter was included as the first among the Apostles and therefore he himself could agree to accept such an assignment. As has been pointed out, these words describe the administration of the sacrament of confirmation. Once more the Apostles acted as a college.

This doctrine, that the Apostles came into existence as a college and acted as a college is further supported from Apocalypse 21:14 where we read: "The city wall had twelve foundation-stones, and on them were the twelve names of the twelve apostles of the Lamb." The twelve Apostles, then, are the twelve foundation-stones. Nor can we say that this is mere imagery. For immediately before in 21:12, the text says that this city of Jerusalem has twelve gates and "on the gates were inscribed the names of the twelve tribes of Israel." Therefore the Apostle John is speaking concretely of the plan of salvation in the Old and New Testaments; it is not a matter then of mere imagery but of concrete reality. From this we see once more how clear is the doctrine of the apostolic college, understood as the foundation of the Church. Now on the foundation the whole house is built.

None of the Fathers should be afraid of this as

dangerous doctrine. For the primacy of St. Peter is in no way denied; indeed it is established by unshakeable arguments. Nor do we speak in an exclusive sense, as though the individual Apostles could do nothing. For there are abundant accounts of what Paul did all by himself. What we are saying is to be understood in a positive but not exclusive sense, *i.e.*, the Apostles acted as a college on major issues even outside of ecumenical councils, as shown above.

This teaching is not only free of danger, but it is an excellent response to the invitation which the Supreme Pontiff has given twice already. He said, for instance, in the opening talk of this session: "For this universal office (*i.e.*, the office of the Pope) may receive more support and help . . . from a more effective and responsible collaboration with our beloved and venerable brothers in the episcopate."

What we have said seems to be a very appropriate response to this invitation of the Pope.

PAUL GOUYON

Coadjutor Archbishop of Rennes,
France

8

Collegiality in Early Church Tradition

Both truths, the primacy of the Roman Pontiff and the collegiality of the bishops, seem to draw their origins from the very earliest times. Then, in the course of the centuries, both of them move along parallel to one another, so that whenever one issue is discussed, the other is immediately raised. At least this is true of the period we are considering, namely, the tradition of the Church in the second and third centuries. With this introduction, let us direct our attention to three kinds of facts which are found in the period under consideration: *First,* letters written by famous bishops to Christians and Churches far away from them; *secondly,* local meetings of bishops which were a kind of prelude to the first Council of Nicaea; *thirdly,* the collegial character of the consecration of bishops:

(1) *Ancient letters of bishops.* Paul wrote to the Christians in the city of Rome, before he had taught them the Gospel by word of mouth, with-

59

out anyone denying him the right to do so, least
of all Peter himself, who on the contrary, praises
him for it in his second epistle. In similar fashion
no one censured Ignatius of Antioch at the end
of the first century for giving advice to the
Churches in Asia and giving fatherly encouragement to Polycarp of Smyrna, a younger brother
bishop.

Ignatius wrote also to the Romans themselves,
though with a certain solemnity and more than
ordinary reverence.

Polycarp too, in the middle of the second century, sent letters to the Philippian Christians.

Some years later Dionysius of Corinth sent
exhortations to the seven Churches of Asia.

Now none of these bishops wrote these letters
out of mere courtesy, but rather to warn their
readers, or to put them on their guard and not in-
frequently because the readers themselves have
asked for their advice.

How could this way of acting make sense if the
authors of the letters were not themselves aware
of the responsibility which they shared with the
bishops of those Churches?

At the same time Clement of Rome spoke to
the faithful of Corinth and used words which point
to a special authority; from this we can legiti-
mately argue to the existence of a power which
in its own order is quite unlimited.

(2) *The first local meetings.* At the beginning
of the second century, the bishops meet and hold
local councils. These first councils are indeed due
to the Roman Pontiff Victor, called to settle the
so-called Easter problem. The bishops treat this

issue not only at Ephesus with Polycrates but everywhere else in the Christian world as well. To prevent the controversy from turning into a bitter conflict some bishops, Irenaeus of Lyons, for instance, turn to the Roman Pontiff, thus acknowledging his authority. The particular tradition of each Church is judged or attacked or defended by the bishops acting as a college. Afterward regional councils are held throughout the whole third century, in the city of Carthage, for example, of Iconium and Alexandria. After the persecutions come to an end, meetings of bishops are held more frequently and especially that famous meeting at which the Roman Pontiff presided through his own legates, the Council of Nicaea.

If the bishops are called in this way to deal with all kinds of issues, even those which do not directly concern each one's own Church but are matters affecting the whole nation or the universal Church, and if their authority to act in this way is never challenged, is it not evident that this is because they all as a united group under the Roman Pontiff as their head, bear a "concern for all the Churches"?

(3) *The collegial character of the consecration of bishops.* From the very earliest times episcopal consecrations were performed not merely by one bishop but by several.

The *Apostolic Tradition* of Hippolytus witnesses explicitly to this fact at the beginning of the third century. "When he has been named, let him, with the presbytery and such bishops as may be present, assemble . . . While all give their consent, the bishops shall impose their hands upon him."

Different translations were made of this text into various languages and it had great influence, especially in the city of Alexandria.

In its fourth canon the Council of Nicaea also has these more specific directions: "It is proper for the bishop to be ordained above all by all those bishops who are in the province. If this should be difficult, at the very least there should be three who come together, and the bishops who are absent should also join in the decision and express their consent in writing." The number is required, then, not to provide a more elaborate ceremony, but because the new bishop is entering into the college of those bishops together with whom he will have equal rights and duties.

To this rule there was no exception. It is in effect from the beginning of all liturgies, although the attitude toward imposing hands differs. Indeed, for many centuries, the Roman Pontiff himself followed this rule when he consecrated bishops. If afterward he performed the rite alone, the explanation is that in his person the whole body of bishops was authentically represented. The modern practice has returned by a different route to the ancient rite. It is well-known that after the prescriptions promulgated by Pius XII, those bishops who take part in a consecration are not named as "assistants" (as was true in the late period at the end of the thirteenth century) but true "co-consecrators".

Facts such as these seem to clearly prove how ancient the notion of collegiality is. So it is not surprising that the holy Fathers speak of it: the order of bishops (in Tertullian, whose meaning is quite precise), the body of bishops, the college of bishops (in Cyprian and Optatus). "If we pastors are many" says Cyprian, "it is a single flock that we feed . . . and we should gather all the sheep together and care for them."

We conclude therefore that the collegiality of bishops, which has its basis in Scripture itself, became a living practice in the Church immediately after the death of the Apostles, just like the pontifical primacy, from which it cannot be separated.

But it is also true that the Holy Father spoke in these terms in the opening discourse of this session: "Here, around him who is last in time and merit, but identified with the first apostle in authority and mission, the successor of Peter, you are gathered, Venerable Brothers, you who yourselves are apostles, descended from the apostolic college and its authentic successors."

MICHAEL DOUMITH

Maronite Bishop of Sarba,
Lebanon

9

The
Significance of
Episcopal Consecration

According to the general doctrine on the sacraments, it is certainly true that a sacrament imparts to him who receives it a grace which works unto his own justification, but this grace works also by a special title unto the fulfillment of that office toward which the sacrament is oriented.

The practice of the early Church and liturgical books make it clear that this exercise of the office of episcopacy is not confined merely to the power of sanctifying the flock committed to its care, to which the powers of teaching and governing the flock would be closely joined, but that episcopacy contains in itself and as one unity the threefold power of sanctifying, teaching, and governing the flock:

(a) *Ancient church practice*: It is apparent from the fact that a bishop can exercise his office immediately after consecration, with no other condition intervening, that all episcopal privileges and prerogatives flow from the very fact of his consecration. He who is consecrated is made a teacher, an authentic herald of the Gospel; he is made a priest, having the power to ordain other priests; he is made a pastor of the flock, or a member of that episcopal college possessing succession from the Apostles. This has in fact been acknowledged by the recent oriental code (can. 396, 2): "Bishops possess jurisdiction and the right to income as soon as they have received episcopal ordination." Under the Latin law, such jurisdiction and rights are reserved to be granted only after canonical installation (CIC 349).

(b) *Liturgical books:* The liturgical books in which are set forth the meaning of the sacrament and the mind of the Church clearly state that the episcopal office, which is conferred at consecration, contains all episcopal prerogatives without any restriction or distinction.

In the Leonine sacramentary we read: "Grant unto them the episcopal throne to rule your Church . . ."

In the Coptic ritual: "Pour out your grace upon your servant whom you have chosen as a bishop to feed and nourish the flock . . ."

In the Antiochene ritual: "Send the Holy Spirit upon your servant that he may nourish and look after the Church . . . and give to him all the powers which you gave to the Apostles of your only-begotten Son . . ."

If these words mean what they say, it must be said that the office of nourishing the flock contains as a single unity and to an equal degree the powers of sanctifying, teaching, and governing. In a word, it contains the apostolic power.

If any sort of delegation of this power is needed, it is already contained in the act of consecration itself. According to the above liturgical books, consecration is done "for a Church" (even today it is made for a Church, even though the Church be destroyed), and in ancient times any consecration made without reference to a definite Church is altogether prohibited (Conc. Chalced. can. 6).

What then must we say of that canonical appointment or delegation which today in the Latin law is what confers jurisdiction? It surely does not confer grace, and hence does not belong to the sacramental order. Does it belong to the apostolic heritage, so that it may be said to confer apostolic power? If we regard the traditions, teaching, and thinking of the Oriental Church—a thing of great importance for ecumenism—we must say that the canonical appointments put forth by the Church are merely for the practical management of the episcopal powers, which have been or are to be received by consecration. The appointment determines, for the sake of the common good, the conditions for the legitimate exercise of the episcopal power. But the power is in itself apostolic and divinely given; it is neither conferred nor removed by the appointment. For that which is divinely given cannot be taken away by human volition, nor can it be humanly provided if it be lacking. The limitations, therefore, and the reservations and severe penalties (to the episcopal power), which for the sake of the common good can and even ought to be invoked, affect merely the legitimacy of the exercise of these powers.

Thus does the Church appear as an institution of divine origin, essentially sacramental, whose manifest purpose is to encourage communion between God and men, through the mediation of the inheritance committed to it by Christ, without the interposition of any human will.

JOSEPH DESCUFFI

Archbishop of Smyrna,
Turkey

10
Papal Infallibility
in the Church

Since the issue of the infallible teaching office of the Church and of the Supreme Pontiff is of supreme importance for the unity which is to be achieved, I wish to propose that it be dealt with in a special paragraph with the title "The Teaching Office of the Church". In this paragraph there should be a clear and exhaustive explanation of the privilege of infallibility and especially of this statement of the First Vatican Council which seems to me to be equivocal:

"The definitions of the Roman Pontiff are of themselves (*ex sese*) infallible . . . and not from the consent of the Church."

Before going any further, may I preface my remarks with a few ideas which were explained in the First Vatican Council by the final "*relator*" of the Deputation on Faith, the reverend Council Father Gasser: "Another reason why we do not exclude the cooperation of the Church is that the infallibility of the Roman Pontiff is not something which comes to him by inspiration or revelation but by the help of God. It follows from this that the Pope, because of his responsibility and the seriousness of the matter, is bound to use appropriate means to properly search out and suitably express the truth; such means are councils or even the advice of bishops, cardinals, theologians, etc. These means are of course different at different times and we should devoutly believe that in the divine assistance which is given to Peter and his successors by Christ the Lord, the promise is also contained of those means which are necessary and appropriate for assuring an infallible judgment of the Pontiff" (*Mansi* 52, 1213).

It seems to me that the First Vatican Council was right in declaring that the definitions of the Roman Pontiff are irreformable (1) *of themselves (ex sese)* and (2) *not from the consent of the Church,* but that the declaration is unclear especially because of the juxtaposition of numbers 1 and 2, which can give rise to the following false interpretations: In number 1: The Pope by himself is infallible even against the opposition of the whole Church or in the absence of the Church; and in number 2: The whole infallible Church can be opposed to the infallible Pope.

This situation is of course quite unthinkable. These two infallibilities, that of the Pope and that of the Church, though they differ in origin and in the subject in which they are found, cannot be opposed to one another but must be joined together in one and the same infallibility.

The first infallibility has as its subject the Pope and it has its origin in the special promise made

to Peter who answered Christ in the name of all
the Apostles as head of the apostolic college. The
other infallibility is that which the Church has in
defining and proposing, an infallibility which will
always agree with the Pope or assent to him.
Therefore:

(1) *Of themselves (ex sese)* means that a special infallibility comes to the Pope as the head of
the Church from Christ and not "from the assent
of the Church" or from the special gifts of the
Pope such as his knowledge or holiness, as some,
despite the disagreement of the Church, demand
and teach.

(2) *Not from the consent of the Church* means
that the infallibility of the Church is not created
by the Pope but strengthened by him; he is united
to it as its head. But the consent of the Church
may in no way be considered as non-existent or
useless, or passed over in silence.

We already said that infallibility is not some
kind of divine inspiration or revelation. It is a
special divine help which exempts from error but
not from the task of investigating the truth, from
study, that is, and consultation, or other means
which differ with the times.

So when the Roman Pontiff speaks *ex cathedra,*
i.e., as Supreme Pontiff and teacher of the universal Church, and when he *strengthens* his brothers, he cannot fail to make inquiries about the
sense of the Church, consulting the Church either
in Councils or in regional or national Councils, or
through other appropriate means, as has always
been done up to now. The Pope alone does not
constitute the Church; but where the Pope is,

there is the true Church in agreement with him. These two members are inseparable as Head and Body in one and the same infallibility.

Furthermore, when the Pastor and Ruler of the universal or ecumenical Church has a great desire that *unity and charity* rule in all parts of the Church spread throughout the world, he will certainly gladly consent to use that unique means which is the consultation of the universal Church, *i.e.,* today's college of bishops, in a manner fore-ordained by divine Providence.

II

Servant of the
Servants of God

The First Vatican Council defined the dogma
of the primacy of the Roman Pontiff. In some
quarters this definition gave rise to false interpretations which distorted its meaning, turning
the primacy, which is a charism given by Christ
to his Church, into an obstacle to Christian unity.
Now we are convinced that what is an obstacle to
unity is not the teaching itself on the primacy,
which has quite adequate support in Holy Scripture
and the tradition of the Church, but exaggerated
interpretations, and even more, the concrete exercise of the primacy where, to authentically divine
elements and a legitimate ecclesial development,
unfortunate borrowings have been more or less
consciously added which are patterned on forms
of exercising a purely human authority.

The Second Vatican Council, according to the
inspiring words of Paul VI in his opening address
of the Council's second session, aims at clearing
the paths which lead to unity. For this reason it

seems to us that the Council should not be satisfied to repeat what the First Vatican Council had to say on this point since this is already an accepted part of the Church's patrimony. What this Council should do is clarify and complete the words of Vatican I in the light of the teaching about the divine institution and the inalienable rights of the episcopacy. In order to give a more prominent position to the principles which assure *a proper balance* to the doctrine and the practice of the Roman primacy, a balance desired by the divine Founder of the Church himself, we should emphasize the following principles:

(1) It should be clear to all of us that the only head of the Church, the only head of the Body of Christ which is the Church, is our Lord Jesus Christ, and he alone. The Roman Pontiff is the head of the College of bishops just as Peter was the head of the College of Apostles. The successor has not more power than the one whom he succeeds. For this reason it is not appropriate to say of the Roman Pontiff as we say of Christ, in the same way and without distinction, that he is the head of the Church, *"caput Ecclesiae"*.

(2) We completely agree with the explanation given by some of the venerable Fathers, of the foundation of the Church. This foundation is made up not of Peter alone, but of all the other Apostles as well, as is proven by a number of texts in the New Testament. This truth is in no way opposed to the primacy of Peter and his successors, but sheds new light on it. Peter is one of the Apostles, and at the same time head of the College of Apostles. Similarly the Roman Pontiff

is a member of the College of bishops and at the
same time head of the College. The head directs
the body but it is not separate from the body.

(3) It should be clear that the power of the
Roman Pontiff over the whole Church does not
take away from the power of the College of bishops as a whole over the Church as a whole—a
College which always includes the Pope as its primate—nor does the Pope's power take the place
of the power of each bishop in his diocese. Every
canonical delegation of authority within the limits
of a diocese comes from the bishop of the diocese
and from him only.

Besides, to present this primacy in such a way
that it would be impossible to explain the very
existence of the Eastern Church would be seriously harmful to the doctrine of the Roman primacy and threaten all possibility of dialogue with
the Orthodox Church. Actually the Eastern
Church owes its sacramental, liturgical, theological and disciplinary life to a living apostolic tradition where the intervention of the Roman See occurs as a rare exception.

(4) We must emphasize that the universal
power of the Roman Pontiff, complete though it
is and remains in its own order, is given to him
essentially as head of the whole hierarchy and
precisely to enable him to fulfill this primatial act
of service.

The "You are Peter" of St. Matthew 16:18
should not be separated from the "Lend strength
to your brothers" of St. Luke 22:32. Furthermore, this power is pastoral in character and
strictly personal. It is pastoral by nature in this

sense that it is not a prerogative of command merely for the sake of command. It is a ministry, a service, a *diakonia,* a pastoral charge, as His Holiness Pope Paul VI has well emphasized. This power is of a personal character and since it remains such, cannot be delegated in any way.

(5) It should be clear that neither the naming of bishops nor their canonical commission are reserved *by divine right* to the Roman Pontiff only. What was a *contingent fact of the Christian West* should not be made a rule for the universal Church or a matter of doctrine.

Thus purified of exaggerations of doctrine and practice, the primacy of the Roman Pontiff not only ceases to be the principal stumbling block to Christian unity but becomes the principal force which calls for and sustains this unity. It is absolutely indispensable as the center of unity for the Church. Christians cannot be grateful enough to the Lord Jesus for this ministry which he has established in his Church.

PART II
Renewal
of the Church

POPE PAUL VI
Bishop of Rome

I
The Task

The same hopes can also be entertained on another chief subject of the Council's deliberations, that, namely, of the renewal of the Church. This too, in our opinion, must follow from our awareness of the relationship by which Christ is united to his Church.

We have just spoken of the bride of Christ looking upon Christ to discern in him her true likeness. If in doing so she were to discover some shadow, some defect, some stain upon her wedding garment, what should be her instinctive, courageous reaction? There can be no doubt that her primary duty would be to reform, correct and set herself aright in conformity with her divine Model.

Reflect upon the words Christ spoke in his priestly prayer as the hour of his Passion pressed close upon him: ". . . I sanctify myself that they also may be sanctified in truth" (John 17:19). To our way of thinking, this is the essential attitude, desired by Christ, which the Second Vatican Council must adopt.

It is only after this work of internal sanctification has been accomplished that the Church will

be able to show herself to the whole world and
say: "Who sees me, sees Christ," as Christ said
of himself: "He who sees me sees also the Father"
(John 14:9).

In this sense the Council is to be a new spring,
a reawakening of the mighty spiritual and moral
energies which at present lie dormant. The Council is evidence of a determination to bring about a
rejuvenation both of the interior forces of the
Church and of the regulations by which her canonical structure and liturgical forms are governed.
The Council is striving to enhance in the Church
that beauty of perfection and holiness which imitation of Christ and mystical union with him in the
Holy Spirit can alone confer.

Yes, the Council aims at renewal. Note well,
however, that in saying and desiring that, we do
not imply that the Catholic Church of today can
be accused of substantial infidelity to the mind
of her divine Founder. Rather it is the deeper
realization of her substantial faithfulness that fills
her with gratitude and humility and inspires her
with the courage to correct those imperfections
of human weaknesses.

The reform at which the Council aims is not,
therefore, a turning upside down of the Church's
present way of life or a breaking with what is
essential and worthy of veneration in her tradition. It is, rather, an honoring of tradition by
stripping it of what is unworthy or defective so
that it may be rendered firm and fruitful. Did not
Jesus say to his disciples: "I am the true vine,
and my Father is the vinedresser. Every branch
in me that bears no fruit he will take away; and

every branch that bears fruit he will cleanse, that it may bear more fruit"? (John 15:1-2).

This verse is a good summary of the perfecting process which the Church today desires, above all as regards her interior and exterior vitality. May the living Church be conformed to the living Christ. If faith and charity are the principles of her life, it is clear that no pains must be spared to make faith strong and joyful and to render Christian instruction and teaching methods more effective for the attaining of this vital end.

The first requirement of this reform will certainly be a more diligent study and a more intensive proclamation of the Word of God. Upon this foundation an education of love will be built up. We must give the place of honor to love, and strive to construct the *Ecclesia caritatis* if we would have a Church capable of renewing herself and renewing the world around her. This indeed is a tremendous undertaking.

Love must be fostered because it is the chief and root of the other Christian virtues: humility, poverty, religion, the spirit of sacrifice, fearless truth, love of justice, and every other force by which the new man acts.

At this point the Council's program broadens to take in immense fields. One subject of the greatest importance is that of the sacred liturgy. The first session of the Council devoted long discussions to this subject. We hope that the matter will be brought to a happy conclusion in the second.

Other fields will also receive the earnest attention of the Council Fathers. However we fear that the brief time at our disposal will not permit us to treat them all as fully as they deserve and that it will be necessary to treat them in a future session.

ERNEST PRIMEAU

Bishop of Manchester,
United States

2

Responsible Freedom
of the Layman

In the outstanding address which the Supreme
Pontiff gave at the beginning of the Council he
emphasized its pastoral importance for the relationship between the hierarchy and the laity. In
following this lead we should keep in mind, above
all when we discuss the laity, the already growing
concern of laymen about their specific role in the
apostolate of the Church. If we fail to do this, all
that the council proposes or decrees will fall on
deaf ears, and with good reason.

We should certainly avoid the danger of general statements, yet we can safely say that today's
layman, aware of his own abilities, will no longer
put up with being treated as a passive member
submitting blindly to the authority of the Church,
as a "silent sheep".

On the contrary, there are a good many of the
Christian faithful, well-informed in many areas,
who ask to be heard when issues come up in which
they have some special competence which the

clergy frequently lacks. They eagerly desire to take part in the apostolic work of the Church and they certainly have the full intention of acting under the direction of the hierarchy, but not without being heard by the hierarchy in those areas where they have special competence; in these matters they expect the hierarchy to trust them.

They have a deep love of Holy Mother Church and express great reverence and confidence in legitimate authority. But at the same time they are aware of their own dignity and ability, not only in temporal affairs but also in those matters which pertain to the interior life of the Church. What they particularly consider to be altogether necessary is open dialogue between themselves and the hierarchy of the Church, so that they will be able to advance the common good of the Church as they should, and make clear the special role of the layman in the apostolate. This ecumenical Council, through God's Providence, has already done much to bring about this dialogue. It has raised great hopes among laymen and has provoked many questions, among them this very important one: what is the proper place of freedom and of authority? Unless the Council answers this question about the relation between freedom and authority, there is no doubt that (1) there will be a growing bitterness of laymen toward Church authority. (2) There will be an increase of indifference among laymen, who will passively observe the laws of the Church but take no part in her life and mission. (3) In some cases there will unfortunately even be apostasy from the faith and the Church. Besides, if the Church is to grow, it needs the help of laymen, especially of intellectuals. But the Church will not be able to use their help and advice at all unless she acknowledges their legitimate freedom of action and their sense of initiative, and unless she is ready to ask their advice with due respect in matters where they are especially competent.

We often speak too much about the need of obedience, reverence, and submission, and do not put enough emphasis on individual responsibility, on freedom of initiative, which must be recognized in laymen in a positive spirit; after all, they are members of the Mystical Body of Christ. They should not constantly be lectured about their duty of subjection and reverence as if their whole vocation were summed up in four words: believe, pray, obey and pay.

We should not forget that the dedicated layman has great respect for the Church and loves her as we love her, but he wants to take an active part in the mission of the Church, to be no longer treated as a mere delegate of the clergy and the hierarchy, but accepted as having his own special place in the mission of the Church as a layman, a man whose special lay role is defined and approved by the Church.

Now all of this will mean very little unless we unhesitatingly declare that we sincerely recognize the competence of laymen, unless we say that we are ready to listen to them, and above all unless we clearly recognize their right to carry on their own spiritual activity, in freedom and in mutual trust, with the authority of the hierarchy. Along this line we bishops should do more to build up and develop "institutes" of some kind so that each diocese will have the machinery through which laymen, especially the more learned among them, will be able to communicate with bishops and pastors. I speak today for laymen and bring their desires to the attention of the Council, and some other bishops have spoken for them in similar fashion. But now I also ask that the laymen themselves be heard by the Fathers, that is, that the "auditors" who are present in this room be heard as spokesmen for all of the laity.

JOSEPH HOEFFNER

Bishop of Munster,
Germany

3

The Lay Apostolate and the Principle of Subsidiarity

I have two observations:

(1) The lay apostolate consists above all and principally *not* in fulfilling tasks assigned to the laity by the hierarchy, but in the example of a truly Christian life and the acceptance of responsibility to renew the temporal order in accordance with the principles of justice and love. This order is of great importance for the salvation of souls both in political matters and in social and economic matters. For social and political conditions are often so contrary to justice and love, that many men find it scarcely possible to lead a truly Christian life, and stubbornly reject Christ and the Church. So the renewal of this order is an excellent form of the lay apostolate.

(2) The apostolate which deals with the temporal order itself and seeks to imbue it with a

Christian spirit normally is the special responsibility of the layman, so that in this task he has a larger role than the cleric, whose first responsibility is that of preaching the word of God and dispensing the divine mysteries. In the relation of the faithful to the Church hierarchy the *principle of subsidiarity* should be followed, a principle which the encylical *Quadragesimo Anno* calls "a principle of the utmost importance". Furthermore, Pius XII explicitly declared that the principle of subsidiarity holds in every society, even in the Church, as long as her hierarchical structure remains intact (Allocution of Feb. 2, 1946). This means that those things which parish priests can do by themselves should not be taken over by the bishop's curia, and just as those things which— leaving the hierarchical structure of the Church intact—can be done by bishops or bishops' conferences should be left to them, *so also* those things which the layman can accomplish on his own initiative and responsibility should not be taken over by the clergy, always with the proviso that the hierarchical structure of the Church is preserved.

CARDINAL PAUL-EMILE LEGER

Archbishop of Montreal,
Canada

4

Holiness of All in the Church

1. HOLINESS IN THE CHURCH.

As is well-known historically, for a long time in the Church the ideal of holiness for monks (living in the desert or in convents) has been the prototype on which all Christian life has been modeled. While there have been happy results, the inconveniences for secular priests and especially for the laity arising from this adaptation must not be forgotten. The life of lay people is so different from that of monks and religious that sanctity has seemed to them to be unattainable. Many of the faithful have searched in vain for a life according to the Gospels suited to their needs; a great loss of spiritual forces in the Church has resulted.

The laity will welcome happily what the chapter on holiness proposed to them. To give more force to these texts, I would propose the following:

(a) The only precise aspect of lay life that is mentioned is conjugal life. It would be good to show that holiness extends to large sectors of life:

89

in addition to married and conjugal life, which is certainly the most important, mention must be made of all the activities of human life — daily work, political affairs, cultural activities, leisure and recreation—through which and in which holiness is to be developed. Likewise, this search for holiness must be pursued by people of all ages, and also by those who are not married.

(b) The text is ambiguous in that it leaves a doubt about the call of all Christians to the practice of the evangelical counsels. The development of faith and hope also must be mentioned. And since one must speak to all Christians about the evangelical counsels, let it be with the full spirituality of the Sermon on the Mount.

What we call the evangelical counsels also include justice, humility, gentleness, mercy. All these aspects of Christian life are required of men of our times for a renewal of holiness according to the mind of the Church. And thus the holiness of the laity will no longer appear to be tied to the counsels as they are practiced in religious life.

(c) A spirituality truly adapted to the laity can be elaborated only if lay people participate in ever greater numbers in the intellectual life of the Church and devote themselves, in collaboration with clergy and religious, to the sacred sciences and principally to "the theology of terrestrial realities". Research in these matters would make great progress if lay people were invited to teach in faculties of religious sciences and in seminaries.

2. THEOLOGY OF CONSECRATED LIFE.

The life of a religious and other types of consecrated life are of great interest to the Church, and the theology on which such a life is based should be clearly set out. Here are some suggestions:

(a) The return to sources is the heart and center of all theological renewal. To renew the theology of the consecrated life, Holy Scripture and Tradition must be studied better. The three traditional "counsels" do not have the same foundation in Scripture. For many theologians, obedience as a "counsel" poses problems of exegesis; on the contrary, virginity is clearly evident in Scripture and Tradition, and even appears to many as forming in itself a state of consecrated life.

Consequently, before treating of religious life as set out in the present law of the Church, one must first speak of consecrated life in general and stress virginity. The celibacy of the secular clergy thus will appear in its full light.

(b) Many expressions are habitually used for those who take the three vows: "those who live in the state of perfection," "those who are called to the evangelical counsels," "those who are pledged to the imitation of Christ." Such terms appear irreconcilable with the very important affirmation of the schema, according to which all are called to perfection, to holiness and to the imitation of Christ by their very baptismal consecration and profession of faith.

GERARD HUYGHE

Bishop of Arras,
France

5

Evangelical
Perfection

We presuppose as certain three facts which we
all hold: the Lord calls all his disciples to perfection; this perfection is the perfection of faith, hope
and love; in us this perfection is rooted exclusively
in the grace of God. In discussing the ways of
acquiring Christian perfection, we must say something about the commandments, the evangelical
counsels, religious vows, and finally about different forms of the religious life.

The Commandments: Sometimes there is a
way of speaking which to a greater or lesser degree
expresses the false doctrine that Christians have
been given only the commandments, and that
greater demands are reserved for a select few.
This is certainly false and smacks of many of the
heresies of Gnosticism and Quietism.

The teaching of the Lord's Sermon on the
Mount, for instance, is proposed to all Christians,
as also the need of self-denial in following the
crucified Christ, etc.

In these sayings we cannot separate commands

and counsels because at certain times they oblige
all Christians with the force of commandments.
Therefore the perfect and complete teaching of
the Gospel embraces both commandments and
counsels, which are part of every Christian's vocation to holiness in the Church.

Evangelical Counsels: We should avoid three
confusions in dealing with these counsels.

(1) The first confusion would be to speak of
the evangelical counsels in the same way as the
commandments. Both, of course, flow from love,
since the commandments are imposed by God's
will, which we must all obey, while the counsels
are simply proposed to us by Christ, as by a friend,
since they help to perfect love. For the Lord did
not want to lead his disciples so much by multiply-
ing commandments, which, as St. Augustine and
St. Thomas Aquinas point out, "are very few in
the New Testament, but rather by proposing certain counsels (to their supernaturally wise choice)
in accordance with the freedom of the sons of
God".

Both in the New Testament and in the Tradition of the Church, the practice of the counsels
really shows itself to be a school in which spiritual
progress and the freedom of the sons of God are
most effectively learned, and this school of the
counsels is extremely useful for the spiritual needs
of our time and for building up the kingdom of
God.

(2) The second confusion about the evangelical counsels would be to think that they are not
proposed for all Christians but only for a select

few, for religious. This confusion causes the utmost harm to the whole Christian people and to religious themselves. The Lord Jesus proposes his evangelical counsels to all his disciples, in every state of life, so that through these counsels they may move with growing freedom toward the perfection of love, and, with God's grace, arrive at this goal.

(3) The third confusion about the evangelical counsels concerns their subject matter and their number. In the practice of the Latin Church, the evangelical *counsels* and religious *vows* made in community life are very frequently confused or at least not clearly enough distinguished. Now since there are three main vows in this community life, obedience, poverty and chastity, we hear very often that there are also three evangelical counsels, poverty, chastity and obedience.

(a) For in the New Testament the Lord and the Apostles speak of voluntary poverty and voluntary chastity and never of the counsel of obedience. There are other counsels as well, for example those in the Sermon on the Mount which deal with the manner of practicing perfect love. These counsels are proposed to all the disciples in every state of life.

(b) In the first centuries of the Church, there were only anchorites or hermits whose life was especially a practice of voluntary poverty, and virgins or widows living consecrated in voluntary chastity from their youth. But the fourth century saw the beginnings of community religious life in which monks made vows of stability and then of obedience.

(c) Not all Christians enter community religious life, and so they are not bound to any particular obedience, but only to the general commandment of obedience. Yet all of them can practice the counsels of voluntary poverty and voluntary chastity in accordance with the norms of Christian prudence.

(d) Finally, we know from our pastoral experience that even in our own day there are those in the world who are so genuinely Christian that they give up the earthly possessions which are theirs by right, for the temporal needs of the Church or to help the poor in their misery. Even in our day many Christian couples, by mutual agreement, live a life of continence for limited periods. Finally, there are many virgins and Christian women who, while living in the world, offer their virginity or chaste widowhood of heart and body to their Lord. Thus these men and women lead an evangelical life in accordance with only two of the counsels, poverty and chastity.

Therefore it is highly desirable that in the chapter which deals with the vocation to holiness we speak of the counsels of voluntary poverty and voluntary chastity, as proposed by the Lord to all Christians, before we deal with the practice of these counsels in that special community religious life which is established in the Church by the vow of obedience.

Religious Vows: Religious vows with varying degrees of solemnity consecrate in the Church the state of life in accordance with the evangelical counsels. By that consecration they are established everywhere in the Church as a public symbol of the holiness of the Holy Church herself. For this reason, the Tradition of the Church has always highly prized the religious state. All of us, bishops and pastors of Churches, know from experience the very great value of the religious life, and know how spiritually productive those monasteries and convents are where a genuinely religious life flourishes, whether apostolic or contemplative, of men or of women. It is certain that in our day, more than in earlier times, the whole Church demands that all religious give to all Christians an example of the freedom of the children of God in the practice of the evangelical counsels.

Different Forms of the Religious Life: Many religious congregations of men and women have grown up in recent centuries for the active or missionary apostolate. But because of the obligatory force of canon law and traditions, the three vows of religion which grew out of community life have been imposed on them, along with "prefabricated" constitutions in which monastic customs, such as cloister, dominate. What is particularly noticeable is that they give their subjects a spirituality modeled on that of contemplatives. The missionary dimension is not found in this spirituality, with the consequence that the soul is torn in two directions.

We do not mean to downgrade the traditional forms of religious life, but neither do we want to close the door on new forms which the Holy Spirit wants to introduce. We especially want to help active congregations to find a unified spirituality which is suited to them and draws its inspiration from their apostolic life.

IGNATIUS ZIADE
Maronite Archbishop of Beirut,
Lebanon

6

Pastoral Need of Permanent Deacons

1. I am speaking exclusively on the practical pastoral level. The importance of the diaconate should not be considered only in the circumstances of the Western world but in relation to the missions as well and to some very extensive regions with few priests and many faithful or catechumens such as Latin America.

In the *Annuario Pontificio* for 1963 the diocese of La Vega has 800,000 faithful with only forty-six priests, about 17,000 faithful for each priest, without making any allowances for priests who are old, sick, chaplains, teachers, or working in the chancery office. In Brazil some of the parishes are as large as four thousand square miles with twenty churches and a single priest as pastor. In some missionary fields the missionary can visit the villages only once in three months and sometimes only once a year and the only person he leaves behind to watch over the Christians and catechumens is a lay catechist.

2. In these last cases very serious problems arise because of the prolonged absence of priests in these immense regions. How can we provide spiritual help and train these multitudes of believers to a life worthy of the Christian name?

Meanwhile Christians are reduced to an abject poverty in their supernatural life when they are deprived of all liturgical worship, of the reading of Sacred Scripture, of the eucharistic Presence in their villages, unable to adore and to receive the eucharistic Body of Christ, without any participation in public prayers. To put it briefly, through no fault of their own they are cut off from all community life of the Church. Many of them die without consolation, without Viaticum, and without even the minimum presence of the hierarchy in its lowest sacramental grade.

The restoration of permanent deacons could provide a partial remedy for these needs and others as well.

3. It is not a question of restoring permanent deacons in all Churches, but only where there is urgent need. Nor is it intended to be a stage toward the priesthood, which remains intact with all its obligations and conditions. Permanent deacons are not meant to make the priesthood superfluous but are to help the priest and remain under his watchful care and authority.

4. What is proposed therefore is a diaconate which will be a fixed state of life, even a permanent state, to serve those communities of the Church where there is no priest.

It will be the responsibility of the deacon to take care of the Church, and open it up, to administer solemn baptism, to reserve, adore and distribute the Eucharist, to administer Viaticum to the dying and console them in their last agony, to bless the faithful in public worship with the Blessed Sacrament or the Cross or the images of saints, to celebrate at stated times sacramentals such as the blessing of water, ashes, palms, candles, fields, etc.

He will have the responsibility of reading the Sacred Scriptures to the faithful and explaining the catechism and of giving sermons in a way the bishop shall decide, of assisting at marriages and blessing them in the name of the Church, of instructing children and preparing all the faithful to receive the Sacred Eucharist in a living manner.

Finally it will be his responsibility to preside at the funeral and burial of the faithful departed. Briefly, he will be a living sign in the midst of Church communities in the villages and towns. He will prepare for the coming of the priest on those few but extremely important liturgical days on which the eucharistic sacrifice is celebrated.

5. Such a deacon evidently must prepare himself by a profoundly Christian life in the congregation of the faithful, through the sacraments and much prayer. He will be an older man whose moral life is so exemplary that there will be nothing in his life to contradict the sacred ministry he exercises in the community.

The bishop will choose one of the more devout and prudent men from a certain congregation who already enjoys the honor and respect of the more responsible part of the community, a man who acts in such a way that he is an example of Christian life for the faithful; he will thus be named by the bishop by a spontaneous choice.

He will not be raised to the diaconate unless he freely and fervently answers the call of the bishop who calls him, delegates him for the needs of souls and consecrates him with a true sacramental ordination. He will be genuinely and completely a deacon in an unqualified sense, with no intention of rising to the priesthood unless he undertakes all the normal seminary preparation and all the obligations of the priesthood without any diminution.

6. Here are the answers to some objections against the restoration of a permanent diaconate distinct from the priesthood:

(a) A permanent deacon can and often should keep his own profession which will support him and his family so that he will in no way be a burden on the faithful.

(b) He will not spend long years in seminary study like other clerics, and will not be bound to extended studies unless the bishop intends to give him the ministry of the Word.

(c) He will not be bound to recite the divine office.

(d) He will not be bound to celibacy as is the priest and the deacon on the way to the priesthood in the Latin Church. And if the wife of a permanent deacon dies, he may marry again.

7. *Conclusion:* These deacons are to be chosen carefully to serve villages or localities which are without priests. It follows that where there are many vocations to the permanent diaconate it is

not easy at present to find vocations to the priesthood.

But later, when the deacons will have prepared a more deeply Christian life and a new, better instructed generation of Christians, then there will be many true priestly vocations.

Finally, where worker priests have had little success in their apostolate to the workingman, deacons, who will be fathers of families, by being and remaining workers, will be able to succeed.

CARDINAL LEON SUENENS

Archbishop of Mechlin-Brussels,
Belgium

7

The Theology of the Diaconate

I wish to speak in favor of restoring a permanent diaconate. Those who have spoken against it seem at times to have forgotten that this is a question touching the very structure of the Church.

1. We should not begin from a kind of naturalistic realism but from a *supernatural realism,* from a lively faith in the sacramental character of the diaconate.

I do not want to stress those issues which are still open questions, such as the pericope dealing with the election of Stephen and the other six (Acts 6:3-6).

However, some things are certain and clearly evident in the New Testament, from the first apostolic Fathers (especially Clement of Rome and Ignatius of Antioch), from the constant tradition which followed, and from the liturgical books of both East and West.

(1) From the time of the apostolic and sub-

apostolic Church, certain of the charisms of the sacred ministry were attributed in a specific and fixed way to a grade distinct from the priesthood.

(2) This grade seems to have been set up especially to provide direct help for the bishop (a) in the care of the poor and the proper direction of the community (b) for what might be called the communitarian preparation of the local Church (especially by brotherly love), and for its liturgical preparation *in the breaking of bread* (Acts 2:42; 4:32-35; Heb. 13:16) to build a real religious community.

If anyone does not see this task of preparation of the community to be a Church as something sacred and necessarily liturgical in its nature, apparently he does not understand the Church as she really is, founded on the sacraments, and this through charisms conferred by the sacrament of orders.

To say that the tasks which are suggested for deacons could just as well be given to laymen is not a valid argument against restoring the diaconate.

It is not a matter of giving these external tasks in any way at all or to any one of the faithful (tasks such as leading prayer, giving catechetical instruction, undertaking social work); these tasks should be given only to him who objectively and adequately has the necessary graces, so that in building a true community there will be no lack of supernatural efficacy. Unless this is true the Church cannot be a true supernatural society, the true Mystical Body of Christ, built up harmoniously on those ministries and graces which the Lord has foreordained.

Furthermore it is not enough to have those gifts and graces which even good laymen may possess through the sacraments of baptism and confirmation and an authentic supernatural spirit.

Since other gifts have been foreordained which are more specifically suited to fulfill the community ministry, they should not be neglected. The Christian community has the right to profit by such gifts which are part of the Church's heritage.

2. Taking these theological principles as a basis, let us see what the actual situation is in different parts of the world.

We hear opposite opinions on this issue. But the objections which have been made to the restoration of the diaconate, though they may have some force in certain circumstances, do not hold everywhere and for all people.

Therefore, it is not up to this Council to make a decision which applies everywhere, or to say that the diaconate is or is not necessary for the whole Church. All the Council should do is explicitly envisage at least the possibility of such a stable ministry, not for the whole Church, but only for those regions in which (with the consent of the proper authority) the legitimate pastors consider this restoration to be necessary if the Church is not to decline but grow and flourish.

This is the question put to the conscience of each one of us, Venerable Fathers: will we, by a merely negative decree, refrain from excluding the possibility of this sacred order as a means foreordained by God, used by the Church for many centuries and now extremely necessary for the renewal of the Church?

According to God's plan, the bishop receives from God the fullness and supreme power of the sacred ministry and likewise receives the commission to establish all those supernatural communities which are necessary for his people.

Therefore the bishop has the power of giving to other ministers a share in his powers adequate to deal with the structure of his people and the circumstances of time and place.

The practical need of the diaconate is evident especially in two cases: (1) when there is a very small community forced more and more to live in the diaspora, *i.e.*, separated from every other group of Christians either because of a difference of religion or vast geographical spread or political circumstances; (2) when there are immense throngs of people, especially in the suburbs, for whom it is necessary to restore some awareness of the Church as a family.

There are situations, therefore, in which the Church is given an opportunity to show herself as missionary in the correct and full sense of the word, ready to allow different solutions for different regions as long as they are all compatible with the structure given her by God.

In such cases I would say that the good of the people is the decisive criterion.

3. What we have said so far is an answer to the principal objection against this proposal, namely, the fear that by opening the diaconate to married men, the law of sacred celibacy will be

weakened and at the same time the number of vocations to the priesthood will decrease.

But if the diaconate is a gift, if it is a grace, and if the legitimate pastors think it appropriate and opportune to draw from this heritage of grace, then the restoration of the diaconate could in no way diminish the fullness of Christ in the Christian community, but rather should augment it.

The precious witness of clerical celibacy should certainly be protected, in accordance with the ancient and venerable practice of the Latin Church.

But a diaconate with a certain clearly defined relaxation of the law of celibacy is not contrary to this practice. Instead of the negative results which some greatly fear, we may instead hope for quite a few advantages: it is not evident why the number of vocations to the priesthood should diminish. This is an a priori assumption. On the contrary, priestly vocations might well increase in communities which are knit together more closely through deacons, prepared by them and more effectively vitalized by their charisms; priestly vocations themselves will consequently be more sincere and genuine and better tested; perfect chastity *for the kingdom of heaven* will be given greater luster and afford a fuller witness.

In order, then, to conclude on a practical note, I propose that the Fathers be asked to consider this suggestion: Where episcopal conferences judge the restoration of a permanent diaconate opportune, they should be free to introduce it.

DENIS E. HURLEY

Archbishop of Durban,
South Africa

8

Pastoral Cooperation Between Bishop and Priests

By the very nature of his ministry, the bishop is supposed to teach, sanctify, and rule. But if we look at what actually happens in practice, what do we see? It is not the bishop but the priest who carries out practically all of the actual day by day ministry of teaching and sanctifying.

And certainly to 99% of his flock the bishop seems an unfamiliar distant figure, unknown on the personal and human level. His task is to lay down the general lines of policy, to bring together and organize the affairs of the diocese, to coordinate the various new projects which are begun; but he very frequently has no direct hierarchical influence on his flock; he does practically everything in the diocese through its priests. For the priests are the hands and feet, the eyes and ears of the bishop, indeed, they are even his voice. And just as no one can act without using the organs of his body, so the bishop, in whatever he wants to initiate, in all that he may hope to do, depends fully and completely on his priests to put his ideas into effect. We all know how much it depends on the way a priest reads out his pastoral letters whether the bishop's words will resound like an archangel's trumpet, or drone on like the columns of a telephone directory.

From all this it is clear that the bishop fulfills his threefold responsibility of teaching, sanctifying and ruling above all by the *leadership* he gives to his priests. Since modern circumstances make it practically impossible for him to have direct contact with his flock, the overriding concern of the bishop should be to provide his priests with pastoral leadership. For he should direct his priests, give them organization, inspiration, encouragement and help. Should anyone object that such a matter belongs to the practical order and does not belong in a dogmatic constitution, my answer is that a dogmatic constitution should pay attention to *facts*. And the principal fact which bears on the ministry of bishops (especially their ministry of teaching and sanctifying) is that in our time these ministries are usually not carried out by bishops but by priests; from this it follows that the principal duty of the bishop is to provide leadership and stimulation.

I admit that in all of this I speak as one less wise, since I know that I am unable to show the precise nature of this task of leadership. Nevertheless it is clear to me that this is a matter of supreme importance. For I believe that if in recent decades the Church seems to have been slow

in responding to the exhortations of the Supreme
Pontiff on the social apostolate, on the missions,
the lay apostolate, and the catechetical and liturgical renewal, the main reason is that we bishops
have fallen short in fulfilling our role of leadership. For we have not known how to pass on the
message of the Pope's encyclicals to our priests
as a living teaching so that they would be able to
communicate it in similar fashion to the people
of God. It is a lamentable fact that the initiative
for Catholic renewal has frequently come not
from us, but from select groups of priests and
laymen.

Of this, then, I am fully convinced: we should
lay it down as a clear principle that the implementation of this ministry consists principally in providing forceful yet tactful pastoral leadership for
priests, who in their turn, with the cooperation of
religious and laity, will accomplish the task which
we ourselves cannot.

The natural and obvious conclusion to be
drawn from these important reflections is that the
priestly order is of supreme importance in carrying out the ministry of the hierarchy. But I have
no time to develop this point further.

IGNATIUS ZIADE

Maronite Archbishop of Beirut,
Lebanon

9

The Rights of Bishops

My remarks deal with two subjects: the rights of bishops and their powers.

1. *The right to take part in an ecumenical Council.* Since a bishop is incorporated into the college of bishops by his episcopal consecration or sacramental character, and not by nomination or election, all consecrated bishops, and they alone, (this includes titular bishops) have the right to take part in an ecumenical Council and cast a determining vote.

2. *The powers of bishops.* One often hears talk about extending the faculties of bishops. It is not a matter of faculties, but of true *powers* rooted in the sacrament of episcopal ordination itself. In the beginning things were different. Bishops were not given powers, whether ample or minimal. The bishops were and are true successors of the Apostles, true vicars of Christ, true pastors, true teachers of the faithful, true rulers of souls. They were never vicars of the Roman Pontiff nor

his delegates in shepherding the flock. But in the course of time their real powers were diminished for many reasons, especially these three:

(a) *Because of general laws.* Almost all the laws of the Church are general laws; in other words, they are made by the Supreme Pontiff or general councils. Therefore only the lawgiver and his successor can dispense from these laws, even in particular cases. Yet these general laws are necessary for the unity of the universal Church.

(b) *Because of reservations* made by the Apostolic Roman See, and these reservations are necessary for the common good.

(c) *Because of our weakness.* In many questions not the little flock, but the pastor with little courage runs to the supreme authority, even in small matters, because he does not know what he may and what he may not do. The answer comes back "We grant you the faculty this time or for three years" and then it becomes a law for the whole world. What should be said is "The chief doesn't bother with trifles".

For all these reasons the bishop, who is a true pastor by divine right with regular and direct power over all the faithful of his flock, may not read or keep a forbidden book, celebrate Mass outside a Church or reserve the Blessed Sacrament in his own chapel. He may not even permit a layman, a member of Christ, a temple of the Holy Spirit and a spiritual priest, to do the first laundering of purificators, palls and corporals!

At present bishops do not know what they may and what they may not do in the care of souls.

I conclude therefore by humbly proposing three changes:

(1) All consecrated bishops, and only consecrated bishops are members of an ecumenical council with the power of casting a determining vote.

(2) The Roman Pontiff reserves certain cases and questions to himself, and other specified cases and questions to Patriarchs, patriarchal synods, and bishops' conferences. Apart from these reserved cases bishops may act freely in their dioceses.

(3) Residential bishops may dispense from general laws in particular cases and for a specified period.

CARDINAL PAUL-EMILE LEGER

Archbishop of Montreal,
Canada

10
Bishops and Evangelical Simplicity

It is most timely that, recalling the words of Christ, the bishop's office is described principally as one of service. In order that the importance of this teaching may be immediately evident, I suggest that the title of the chapter itself should contain the word "service".

The sections on the bishop following in the footsteps of Christ, who came to serve, and not to be served, are excellent. But may I conclude by expressing the desire that this spirit of humble service and evangelical poverty may be more manifest in the daily relations of bishops with the faithful and with the world. To provide efficacious help in this direction, I make bold to suggest that a study be made, which would be followed by a set of regulations concerning the insignia, ornaments and titles which we often use against our will and which are harmful to the fulfillment of our pastoral ministry.

I wholeheartedly subscribe to what has been said in this room about the special concern of the Church for the poor. But the continuing use of ancient splendor is an obstacle to working for them in the spirit of the Gospel. Perhaps this splendor was thought to be necessary when some bishops held secular authority as well. But in our time, on the contrary, such display no longer fits into the normal pattern of public life and is out of tune with our spirit.

CARDINAL LEON SUENENS

Archbishop of Mechlin-Brussels,
Belgium

II

Age Limit
for Bishops

My remarks are on the question of relinquishing office.

When the Preparatory Commission, of which I was a member, began to discuss this issue, practically all its members rejected the idea of some legal regulation which would set an age limit. But when this discussion, which was long and thorough, came to an end, a very large majority of the bishops, as the Relator has pointed out, voted in favor of such a regulation. And with very good reason, it seems to me.

This is a delicate question, since no one is a good judge in his own case. It is clear that this question involves the theology of the episcopacy. But we should be careful not to invoke certain principles in a one-sided manner and forget about others.

Some of the speakers in this room have called on the principle of the perpetual role of the bishop as father. A father certainly always remains a father, but as the years pass, the sons take from their father's hands more and more of the responsibility for directing the affairs of the family.

Some have called on the principle of indissolubility of the marriage between the bishop and the people committed to his care.

But this Council hall is full of "divorced" bishops, some of them for the second and third time. We should not insist on such principles. And above all we should not forget other principles which are really more decisive. Does not the Gospel itself and apostolic and subapostolic tradition remind us that our ministry is a service for the good of souls?

The whole question, then, comes down to this: what does the salvation of souls and the true service of the diocese require in this matter?

(1) When the matter is seen in this light, the need of some regulation becomes clear. For we all know that if the problem is solved by pious exhortations, nothing is solved: it will be like writing in water. Yet the matter is extremely important, since our Council is one of pastoral renewal.

This renewal must begin with the bishops themselves, including the Cardinals. The Second Vatican Council will go down in history as the Council about bishops. Everything which has been discussed so far is in the direction of greater responsibility assumed by the bishops both in their particular Church and, in their own way, in the universal Church.

Now where there is greater responsibility, greater ability is required. The function of the bishop has taken on new dimensions in our day. It is no longer what it had been for centuries, but the bishop takes on more and more the role of being the vivifying spirit who coordinates all apos-tolic work, the leader and the soul of that *"pas-torale d'ensemble"*, or "group ministry". He is the source of initiative, providing such leadership for the people entrusted to him—diocesan and reli-gious priests, brothers and sisters, those active in the lay apostolate and all the faithful—that they work together with unified force and one spirit to put the whole Church in a state of mission and evangelization.

All of this requires more than ordinary strength and energy.

(2) Furthermore, the sociological develop-ment of the world makes modern life move at a faster and faster pace. Every day new problems arise. The bishop must be constantly on the alert to meet new needs. Now this situation calls for a man who is young in both mind and body, so that he can understand what adaptations are needed and put them into practice. Advanced age automatically puts a gap between the bishop and the world which needs salvation, between him and the clergy, and this does great harm to the spiritual welfare of the diocese.

The very nature of old age makes it impossible at a certain point for the person growing old to be aware of his own inadequacy, because it hap-pens without him realizing it.

(3) To come to a sound judgment on this problem it is enough to consider the state of a diocese where the bishop is quite old. All of us

know such cases. There is no need to dwell further on this point; the evidence is too manifest, distressing, and damning.

(4) We should also remember that a bishop often has to ask an aging priest to resign for the good of the parish or the office he has held. How will this be done if the bishop himself is too old? How can we prevent such a priest from saying, or at least thinking, "Doctor, cure yourself!"?

(5) Furthermore, we should not forget that our faithful are watching very closely and want to see our reaction in this matter. For them, such a proposition from us would be a clear sign of our sincerity in pastoral renewal. We should beware of scandalizing the faithful, especially since in our day, for the common good, there is everywhere an age limit—and lower than 75 years—in the secular world, in universities, in industry, in diplomatic service. If this is necessary in the secular order, why should we not insist on it for the supernatural good of souls. It is quite true that there is a very great difference between a merely human office and a supernatural office like the episcopacy, but the laws of human psychology and physiology remain the same, and the demands of the supernatural common good are far more important than merely temporal needs.

Before coming to a concrete conclusion, let me add these few remarks:

(a) It is clear from the nature of the case that this need for an age limit does not apply to the Supreme Pontiff; the universal good of the Church demands that he remain in office for life.

(b) It is clear that the bishop who gives up his

office has every right to proper support and to everything which befits his state.

(c) It would be possible to make exceptions to the law for those bishops who are now close to the age limit.

(d) Perhaps the sociological situation of the Eastern Churches does not so urgently require a solution of this kind.

With these reservations, may I assert that the good of souls calls not only for advice and persuasion but a genuine legal regulation, though it should be very carefully framed and always subject to the judgment of the Roman Pontiff in really extraordinary cases.

In conclusion, I suggest that even though our Council does not set an obligatory age limit of 75 years, it should *at least* decree that a bishop must *always* be given a coadjutor after that age. The bishop should remain, enjoying great consideration and respect as a revered father in his own house, but the coadjutor should gradually take over the central direction of the whole diocese, with as many faculties as the Apostolic See decides in each case, keeping in mind the greater or lesser incapacity of the bishop.

It seems to me that in this way the various aspects of the problem can be worked out together for that pastoral renewal which we desire as the goal of our Council.

EUGENE D'SOUZA

Archbishop of Bhopal,
India

12

Bishops'
Conferences Today

I speak as a missionary, in the name of eighteen missionary bishops, about the usefulness of bishops' conferences in missionary regions.

It has often been said already that we have been called by Pope John, whose memory will live forever, to adapt the Church to today's needs. The urgency of this need is nowhere more evident than in the missions. The liturgy of the Roman rite, for instance, though beautiful and profound, is something foreign in regions of an entirely different culture, and will remain foreign to them. Who would be better equipped to adapt it than a bishops' conference with the help of experts from that region?

The liturgy schema has very wisely made this provision. I merely remind you of it as an illustration of the general principle.

Bishops' conferences should not be merely some form of collaboration within the framework of existing canon law. They open up much broader horizons. In order to have a full insight into their usefulness it is not enough to study the matter with an administrator's eye. We need a wider vision, a kind of prophetic vision.

Bishops' conferences should look for new forms of incarnating the Gospel of Christ, and the primal sacrament which is the Church, in every people and culture. If we speak of "particular circumstances" we do not go far enough. It is not only the *circum*-stances, the peripheral elements which differ, as though the central and essential reality were everywhere the same. At times there are constellations of reality which are completely original. Although Western techniques are spread over the whole world, are not India, the United States, the Congo, Poland, and Ecuador totally different? In order truly to give flesh to Christ, it is not enough to apply stereotyped formulas everywhere. What is needed above all is laborious study and thought, then steady application of these ideas so that those norms which seem useful may be reduced to practice through the united effort of all. Who but bishops' conferences can do this?

This being the case, Venerable Brothers, no one can fail to see that bishops' conferences need definite juridical status. If these groups are merely consultative and have no true power to legislate, those who have built them have wasted their time. We hope that in the revision of the Code it will be laid down that in certain points of major importance the Church should not be ruled by uniform law, but conferences will be given the authority to deal prudently with the matter. It is also clear that on this point individual bishops will have to go along with the decision made by democratic process. For every kingdom divided within itself shall be laid waste. If bishops paralyze a conference by their individualism or turn it into a debating club, the only remedy will be to be ruled once more from Rome by a uniform law, and thus we shall rapidly return to the situation which prevailed before the Council.

But if bishops are to cooperate gladly and support the decisions of the conference, they must carry on their business in truly democratic and collegial fashion. Let me make a few suggestions on this subject.

Many bishops are evidently opposed to legislative power for conferences either because they are afraid they will fall victim to some kind of tyranny, either of the majority or of the president, or that the whole thing will turn into a bureaucracy, or even that before long it will bog down because it is always run by the same men.

These are legitimate concerns, and so the Council should lay down certain guidelines to guard against such deviations. Each conference should be allowed to work out its own constitution and bylaws, but certain essentials should be safeguarded.

This Council, therefore, should decree that:

(1) The president, the council and the commissions should be elected by the conference through a secret ballot for a specified term, not to exceed five years, the rights of Patriarchs in Eastern rites remaining intact.

(2) All the votes are to be secret.

(3) Decisions should be made by a 3/4 majority.

But if a decision is approved by a 2/3 vote it may be recommended for a three year experiment if the nature of the case permits. When the three years have elapsed, the matter must be dealt with afresh.

I would like to add two important points. The first concerns provincial or regional conferences. Remember that a provincial council is to be held at least every ten years. But was not this law passed when traveling was more difficult? The bishops of my province, indeed of this whole part of India, meet twice a year. Why should only one out of twenty of these meetings be entitled to juridical status?

When I say "my region" please do not forget that India has 460,000,000 inhabitants, and the province where I am metropolitan is three times the size of Italy. You can see why in nations which are immense and have an extraordinary diversity it is very useful to have conferences within the nation which have full juridical status, and why the national conference should be a kind of federation of these provincial councils.

My second point starts from the fact that we want to promote the cooperation of everyone through conferences. Now a large section of the clergy, indeed, a group which is constantly growing, is made of religious. These men always carry a large share of the burden and heat of the day, and sometimes the greater part of it. Just as general superiors of the principal religious orders and congregations have a determining vote in the ecumenical council, so also the members of the permanent council of major superiors, or if the number of bishops is small, at least their president should have a membership with full rights in the episcopal conference.

Venerable Brothers, this is a project of the utmost importance; I hope that my suggestions contribute to it in some positive way.

ELIAS ZOGHBY

Greek-Melchite Patriarchal
Vicar in Egypt

13

The Eastern Churches
and Bishops' Conferences

What I have to say about bishops' conferences
can be summed up in the following four points,
some of which are ecumenically important:

1. The relationship of the Roman Church to
Eastern Orthodoxy grows out of ten centuries of
union, during which she not only *acknowledged*
their collegial and synodal form of government,
but also *lived* according to this pattern together
with the traditional or apostolic Churches of the
East.

Actually, even if we prescind from the great
ecumenical Councils which brought together the
episcopacy of the East and West, under the un-
challenged presidency of the Bishop of Rome, the
Roman Church exchanged synodal letters with
the traditional or apostolic Churches of the East,
letters dealing with problems which concerned
both the local Churches and the universal Church.

In our day, when the Catholic Church is trying
to become more accessible to the communion of

Eastern Orthodoxy, and is preparing for ecumenical dialogue, the only form of church government which the Second Vatican Council can propose to the Churches of the East is synodal governments, *i.e.*, government by genuine bishops' conferences with real power. To speak of conferences which would be purely consultative would forestall the possibility of dialogue.

2. Episcopal synods or conferences in the Catholic Churches of the Eastern rite have been deprived of all real power, which has been put in the hands of the Roman Curia, especially the Sacred Congregation for the Eastern Church. To convince oneself of this, all one need do is consult the new Code of Eastern Canon Law. What this congregation actually does is assume the role of a pseudo-patriarchate.

It is true that the six Patriarchs of the East have been named associate members of the Congregation for the Eastern Church, which already has about thirty members, all of them Cardinals. This solution fails to accomplish anything concrete, and is neither an honorable nor an ecumenical solution.

To take Patriarchs, who by right are the presiding officers of their Synods, and make them secondary and minority members of a Congregation with authority to deal with the affairs of their own patriarchates is actually a condemnation of the synodal form of government.

What should be put in the place of this congregation is a body whose members would be delegates of the episcopal synods or conferences of the Eastern rite Churches.

3. Bishops are the pastors both of Catholic action and the whole apostolate of the laity, and they are the ones who bear the primary responsibility for it. Now this apostolate is no longer limited to the boundaries of definite parishes or dioceses. It is organized on a national or worldwide scale. Only the collective power of the episcopacy will make it possible for them to carry on their pastoral action on the level of national or universal bodies of the lay apostolate, which should be under the control and direction of the bishops.

4. In this room we have heard opposition to collegiality and bishops' conferences with juridical power, based on fear of a dangerous nationalism.

Now we have arrived at a moment in history when nationalism, at least if it is not a narrowly centralized nationalism, is no longer a danger to the universal good, but instead a way of enriching the whole of human society.

Actually, as the young nations progress and gain their freedom we see that the international bodies in which these peoples participate on an equal basis become more vital and important than ever.

Will men of the Church be less largehearted and open than statesmen?

EUGENE D'SOUZA

Archbishop of Bhopal,
India

14

Bishops and the Roman Curia

We have heard in this Sacred Synod that the question of collegiality is not yet settled, and that some of the arguments advanced are therefore invalid and illegitimate. There are two things I would like to say in reply.

(1) Does it not seem a mockery of the Council to say that in discussion no account should be taken of the opinion expressed by 85% of the Council Fathers in a clear vote, especially since anyone who has listened closely to the talks given in recent weeks by our beloved and revered Pope Paul VI, can sense the direction in which his own thoughts tend?

(2) As a missionary, speaking in the name of ten other missionary bishops, I beg you, Venerable Fathers, not to turn this into a juridical question. What concerns us above all is the good of souls, which is the decisive norm.

Pope John, whose memory will live forever, called us together for an *aggiornamento* of the

Church. What does this mean? The Church, as a living organism, must adapt herself to the times, and as long as the essentials remain intact, should not remain changeless forever. In his unforgettable address to the Curia, our beloved Pope Paul VI said that the Curia is no exception to this law. He recalled all the many things which are to its credit, but together with him we openly raise the question of how far we should go in reforming it.

Can we expect any great gain by naming a few bishops as members or consultors of curial Congregations? This would produce nothing more than a superficial difference in something which would remain basically unchanged; it would not be a thorough reform. Unless questions of this kind are clarified, unless, in accordance with the desires of the great majority here present, the power of the Curia is precisely limited, everything will be just as it was before, at least after a few years. If 2,200 bishops, gathered together from all over the world for an ecumenical council, sometimes find it difficult to stand up against certain pressures, what would these few bishops, scattered through the various congregations, be able to do. And the last state will be worse than the first.

We know that some are afraid the increase of powers for the bishops will endanger the unity of the Church. This seems to be a false prejudice, which can be refuted in several ways.

As if decentralization were an obstacle to unity! Or, to put the issue on another level, as if a state with a federal or democratic government had no body of unity!

And we twentieth-century bishops, are we so dangerous, after all? Have we no sense of responsibility for the Church? Are we really incapable of deciding what is good for the Churches entrusted to our care? The Church is spread throughout the world, and in her spiritual, theological and liturgical life, in her pastoral concern, she flourishes even in those lands where she lives in the diaspora. In those regions where serious problems threaten the Church, pastors see more and more clearly that the reason why it is almost impossible to solve these problems is that laws and practical procedure have not been adapted, that, to put it bluntly, a canon law which is the same the world over becomes in their case the letter that kills.

Here we come to the heart of the problem. We cannot confuse unity with that uniformity on which the central body insists.

The Roman Curia, as a centralized power, issuing rather uniform legislation, was certainly extremely useful, especially when kings and governments tried to dominate the bishops they used to appoint, when means of communication were also so slow that the Church had to be held together by very rigid external discipline.

At present bishops are freely appointed almost everywhere in the world by the Supreme Pontiff without interference from civil authority. And—what is most important—means of communication are so easy that they foster unity of minds and hearts, by far the principal bond of union. Television does more to promote enthusiastic love of the Sovereign Pontiff than the acts of certain Congregations. The words of Ignatius of Antioch were never so completely shown to be true: "The Roman Church presides over a universal community of love."

In all sincerity we must admit that at times this love is endangered by the present practices of the Roman Curia: when someone is punished without being heard; when general suspicion is aroused against a well-known writer without saying precisely what is objectionable in his writings and what is praiseworthy; when general regulations are issued which are not suited to local conditions; when a suggestion proposed after mature reflection by the bishops of a certain province, even of a nation, is rejected with a laconic *"non expedit"* —"better not"; when a petition for the dispensation from a marriage which has been celebrated but never consummated drags on for years and years without a solution.

I wish to conclude with one observation.

No one thinks the Roman Curia has to be suppressed or even seriously weakened. But it must be thoroughly reformed. This is one of the fundamental goals which have been set for the Council everywhere in the world. Let us take care, Brothers, that we do not shatter these hopes.

Remember the Fifth Lateran Council, which was held from 1512 to 1517. Whether it was lack of vision or lack of courage, I do not know, but it failed to accomplish the reforms which men at that time hoped for. A few months later, the Church went through the worst crisis in her whole history. Brothers, let us have the courage to give an answer to the needs of our time.

MAXIMOS IV
Patriarch of Antioch,
Syria

15

The
Supreme Senate of
the Catholic Church

It seems to me that if we envisage the Pope in his ministry of primacy to the universal Church surrounded by no other assistance than the congregations, tribunals and offices which together make up the Roman Curia, we fail to meet the real needs of the Church of our time and to face up to the collegial responsibility of the episcopate for the Church.

May I suggest a new solution which seems to me to give a more adequate response to the needs of our times and the sound principles of theology.

Peter with the Apostles is the Pope with the body of bishops. The Pope is also Bishop of Rome, Primate of Italy, and Patriarch of the West. But these qualities—though real—are secondary with relation to his universal primacy.

Since this is so, it follows that when the Pope governs the universal Church, he associates with him, to share his responsibility, the College of bishops who succeed the College of the Apostles, and not the priests, deacons and other clergy of the diocese of Rome. The special curia of Rome, for the diocese of Rome, should not take the place of the College of the Apostles which lives on in the bishops, who are their successors. It is then the task of this Sacred Council to take necessary means to clarify this truth which has been confused by the practice of centuries, and has steadily been obscured by thicker and thicker clouds so that many, even among us, have finally taken the situation to be normal, though it is not normal at all; for the curia of the Bishop of Rome is one thing, and the Apostolic College of the successor of Peter is something else. With the Curia of the Pope in its present state, it is hard for those outside the Catholic Church, and for not a few who are inside, to see the ecumenicity of the Church; instead they see the particular character of a particular Church, to which certain men, a certain history and favorable circumstances have given a heritage of human and material sources having considerable grandeur, power, and wealth. The very fact that Cardinals are appointed for particular Churches of Rome shows well that the Cardinals belong to the particular Church of Rome and not to the universal Church of Christ.

It is obvious that all the bishops of the world cannot be continuously meeting in Council. The concrete responsibility of helping the Pope in the general government of the Church must be given to a limited number of bishops who will represent their fellow bishops. This is the group which could form the true *Sacred College* of the universal Church. It would include the principal bishops of the Church. First of all there would be the residential and apostolic patriarchs who have been recognized by the ecumenical councils of the first centuries; then would come the cardinal archbishops, with the title of their own cathedral and not the title of a parish of Rome; lastly there would be the bishops chosen by the episcopal conferences of each country. This last suggestion should be studied to work out the details. This Sacred College could be called together by the Pope at fixed intervals and when it seems necessary to discuss the general affairs of the Church.

But that is naturally not enough. At Rome there should always be what the Eastern Church calls the *"Synodos endimousa"*, *i.e.*, certain members of this Sacred Apostolic and universal College who would take their turn being at the side of the Pope, their head, who by his right as primate always has the last word. This is where the Supreme Council of the Church will be, the *"Suprema"*, supreme executive and judicial Council of the universal Church. All the Roman offices should be under it. This *"Suprema"* will have a special set of rules to determine its structure. It will radiate Christ throughout the whole world, especially in the pagan world. Since it will not be isolated in a center closed in on itself, the idea will not even occur to it of wanting to monopolize everything, regulate everything, lord it over everything, acting with exaggerated uniformity and, at times, meddlesomeness. It will understand that *the problems of peoples must be settled by these people, and with them, but never without them.*

To sum up, we say that neither the Holy Father nor anyone else in the world, whoever he be, can with his personal aides govern an institution as large as the universal Church, where the interests of Christianity in the whole world are at stake. And all of this is in accordance with the Gospel, for if the Church has been entrusted in a special way to Peter and his successors it has also been entrusted to the Apostles and their successors; and if this government is entrusted to persons who do not have this role by the very nature of the Church, such as personal associates and local clergy, the general good must suffer and real catastrophe could result. History gives us examples of this.

At the present moment, these truths which concern the theology, the structure and the practice of the Church, become urgent and serious problems.

In the countries of Mediterranean civilization of the ancient Roman Empire of the East and West, or in the countries which derive from them, things could carry on for an indefinite period if considerable authority were given to bishops' conferences, which are really a modern form of the historic patriarchates. But in those countries with vast populations like China and India, countries with great and ancient civilizations which have nothing in common with the civilization of the Mediterranean, something more is needed, something which should be worked out with the help of Christianity itself. The same thing should be said about the African Churches, so rich in dynamic forces. There is a great work of radical adaptation which needs to be done so that these

Churches may feel at home in language, mentality, customs and usages. They must feel that Christianity is not something foreign for them, that it could be the soul of their soul. These peoples should enjoy a still greater inner autonomy than that of the Mediterranean countries, while keeping, above all this, the necessary link with the See of Peter. Only what is essential in the structure of the Church should be required of them, as the First Council of Jerusalem decided long ago for the gentiles. After so much very praiseworthy labor, dedication, expense and sacrifice, can we say that Christianity has won the hearts of these people? Yet that is what must be done.

It will be the task of the new Sacred College to shed light on these great problems and, through prayer, study, time and the requisite prudence, to provide the proper solution. The members of the Sacred College who come from all parts of the world and thus have an ecumenical mentality will also be better able to bring this task to a successful conclusion, to give to the Church an organism able to provide capable direction for all peoples within the framework of Catholic unity.

If the Holy Spirit, using as his instrument Pope John XXIII of holy memory, suggested that this Council be held to open the way to dialogue between the Church and the whole world, and if then, after Pope John's death, the Holy Spirit inspired the choice of our Holy Father Paul VI to continue and to organize this divine task, it is because he is always in his Church to guide her and give her life. "Send forth your Spirit and he shall renew the face of the earth."

JOACHIM AMMANN

Titular Bishop,
Muensterschwarzach,
Germany

16

Nunciatures

The Council Fathers have shown their almost unanimous agreement to close the debate on Chapter II of the schema on the Church, which treats of the relations between the Supreme Pontiff and the bishops.

Bear with me, Venerable Fathers, if in this context I venture to add a few remarks about a particular *institution* which should help to foster the cordiality of these relations. The Most Excellent Patriarch Gori has, in fact, already said a little about this subject in speaking of the importance of nuncios and apostolic delegates.

To prevent any misunderstanding, let me begin with these preliminary remarks:

(1) I am not a member of any bishops' conference. However, quite a few of the Council Fathers have expressed their agreement with what I have to say. I have given the names of five of them in writing to the General Secretariat. (I speak because I feel bound in conscience to do so.)

(2) I do not want to assert a thesis but rather to ask a question, following the proverb I heard

so often in Africa: "Kuuliza si kosa" which means "It's no sin to ask."

(3) Nothing is further from my mind than to pass judgment on any individual *persons*. I know the high virtue and merit of my brothers in the episcopate who fill these offices. I speak *exclusively* about the institution itself.

(4) What encourages me to ask this question in connection with Chapter II of this schema is the admonition of our present Holy Father Pope Paul VI. In his allocution of September 29 he said: "The Church wants to look for her model in Christ . . . If after this reflection she should notice any shadow on her countenance, on her wedding garment, what should be her instinctive courageous reaction?" And the Supreme Pontiff himself gives the answer: "There is nothing else to do but to . . . correct herself, to set herself aright in conformity with her divine Model . . ." Thus "the Church will be able to show her face to the *whole world* . . ." Her fidelity to Christ must be more thoroughly tested. "Those weaknesses which spring from human infirmity must be corrected."

It is true that we must in no way overlook the other admonition of the Holy Father: We must be careful not to break with the traditions of the Church "in what is essential and worthy of veneration."

After these preliminary remarks, here are the *questions*:

(1) Is the institution of nuncios, internuncios and apostolic delegates, as "diplomatic representatives of the Holy See" one of those "essential

traditions worthy of veneration" which may in no way be broken?

There are quite a few who think that this institution, to the extent that it imitates the diplomatic institutions of secular powers, should *in our day* be counted among the *shadows* which hide the *true* face of the Church from men of our time.

In the eyes of many people this institution of "diplomatic representatives" makes the Church of Christ *like* secular powers and—in spite of all protestations to the contrary—leads many people, (even Christians) to believe that the Catholic Church is a party on one side or another of political and social disputes.

(2) Should not the question be raised whether the time has come to transfer the religious and ecclesiastical tasks of these "diplomatic representatives" to the Patriarchs, Primates, bishops, or other men chosen for this task by each of the bishops' conferences?

These men would know the traditions, culture, *language,* and mentality of each region much more intimately, and would be able to provide Rome—in the very center and heart of the Church—with much better information about conditions in their own territories.

And this does not in any way deny that genuinely *extraordinary* matters could call for extraordinary measures.

When it comes to handling those questions in which the Church is involved in a hundred ways with *secular* matters, the local or territorial hierarchy would do *better* to delegate such responsibilities to outstanding, that is, competent and expert, laymen. They would be "Confessors" but not (necessarily) "Pontiffs".

(3) Are we compelled by any biblical or theological authority (or by experience) to believe that more trust should be placed in training received in a diplomatic school, than in bishops whom the Holy Spirit has placed to rule the Church of God?

If we are to bring these remarks to a close with a conclusion, let it be that the institutions of which we have spoken—which undoubtedly were praiseworthy in their time and which therefore deserve our respect and gratitude—should be thoroughly reappraised and overhauled (and where necessary, filed away in those cabinets where historical Acta and venerable relics are stored).

PART III
Reunion
of All Christians

POPE PAUL VI
Bishop of Rome

1
The Task

The Council has a third object, one which in the order of spiritual realities is most grave. This too was put before us by Pope John XXIII. It concerns "the other Christians"—those who believe in Christ but whom we cannot happily number among ourselves in the perfect unity of Christ which only the Catholic Church can offer them.

This unity, objectively speaking, should be theirs by baptism. It is something which, virtually at least, they already desire. For recent movements, at present in full development in bodies of Christians separated from us, show clearly two things. The first is that the Church of Christ is one alone and therefore must be unique. The second is that this mystic and visible union cannot be attained except in identity of faith, and by participation in the same sacraments and in the organic harmony of a single ecclesiastical direction, even though this allows for a great variety of verbal expressions, movements, lawful institutions, and preference with regard to modes of acting.

There can be no doubt about the attitude of the Council with regard to these great numbers of separated brethren and of the possibility of multi-

145

plicity in the unity of the Church. This too is one of the characteristics of the Council.

The Council aims at complete and universal ecumenicity. That is at least what it desires, what it prays and prepares for. Today it does so in hope that tomorrow it may see the reality. This Council, while calling and counting its own those sheep who belong to the fold of Christ in the fullest and truest sense, opens the door and calls out, too, in anxious expectation to the many sheep of Christ who are not present within the unique fold.

It is a Council, therefore, of invitation, of expectation, of confidence, looking forward toward a more widespread, more fraternal participation in its authentic ecumenicity.

We speak now to the representatives of the Christian denominations separated from the Catholic Church, who have nevertheless been invited to take part as observers in this solemn assembly. We greet them from our heart. We thank them for their participation. We transmit through them our message—as father and brother—to the venerable Christian communities they represent.

Our voice trembles and our heart beats the faster both because of the inexpressible consolation and reasonable hope that their presence stirs up within us, as well as because of the deep sadness we feel at their prolonged separation.

If we are in any way to blame for that separation, we humbly beg God's forgiveness. And we ask pardon too of our brethren who feel themselves to have been injured by us. For our part, we willingly forgive the injuries which the Catholic Church has suffered, and forget the grief endured during the long series of dissensions and separations. May the heavenly Father deign to hear our prayers and grant us true brotherly peace.

We are aware that serious and complicated questions remain to be studied, treated and resolved. We would wish that this could be done immediately on account of the love of Christ that "urges us on". But we also realize that these problems require many conditions before satisfactory solutions can be reached—conditions which are as yet premature. Hence we are not afraid to await patiently the blessed hour of perfect reconciliation.

Meanwhile we wish to affirm before the observers here present some points in our attitude toward reunion with our separated brethren, with a view that they may communicate them to their respective Christian communities.

May our voice also reach those other venerable Christian communities separated from us, that did not accept the invitation freely extended to them to attend the Council. We believe these points are well known, but it is useful to repeat them here.

Our manner of speaking toward them is friendly, completely sincere and loyal. We lay no snares. We are not motivated by temporal interests. We owe our Faith—which we believe to be divine—the most candid and firm attachment.

But at the same time we are convinced that this does not constitute an obstacle to the desired understanding with our separated brethren, precisely because it is the truth of the Lord and therefore the principle of union, not of distinction or separation. At any rate we do not wish to make of our Faith an occasion for polemics.

Secondly, we look with reverence upon the true religious patrimony we share in common, which has been preserved and in part even well developed among our separated brethren. We are pleased to note the study made by those who seek sincerely to make known and to honor the treasures of truth and of genuine spirituality, in order to improve our relations with them.

We hope that just as they are desirous to know more about our history and our religious life, that they would also wish to make a closer study of our doctrine and its logical derivation from the deposit of divine Revelation.

Moreover we are aware of the enormous difficulties still in the way of this desired union. We humbly put our trust in God. We shall continue to pray. We shall try to give better proof of our efforts of leading genuine Christian lives and practicing fraternal charity. And should historical reality tend to weaken our hopes, we shall try to recall the comforting words of Christ: "Things that are impossible with men are possible with God." (Luke 18:27).

CARDINAL J. HUMBERTO QUINTERO

Archbishop of Caracas,
Venezuela

2

Confíteor

If we keep in mind the expectant hope aroused
in the whole world the moment the news was first
released that this Council would take place, we
will see clearly how important is the subject now
under discussion. For people all over the world
believed that the principal purpose of the Council
would be to restore unity among those Churches
which glory in the Christian name; indeed this still
remains their hope today. So it would be a waste
of time to dwell on the great importance of this
question of ecumenism.

In our time the human race seems to be search-
ing for unity on every level. It is clear that the
scientific discoveries of this age, which make communication between peoples rapid and easy, contribute greatly to this unity. But the most intense
desire for unity is on the spiritual level, even on
the level of religion, so that we may honestly say
that the desire of Our Lord Jesus Christ for one
fold and one shepherd has become universal. Always concerned for the eternal salvation of souls,
the Church wants to work with all diligence to

bring men eventually to this unity; the present schema is evidence of that desire.

The inner renewal of the Church, conversion of heart, and holiness of life are set down in this schema as the foundation required for true ecumenism. In this way the beauty of the Church will shine clearly before all men and draw strangers to her, since beauty has great power of attraction. But beauty, according to the well-known definition is nothing other than the splendor of truth, and therefore the Church should display her treasures of truth, and I speak not only of those truths which are part of the deposit of faith, but also of other truths related to the Church, which certainly include truths of history.

Frequently when we are discussing the origins of those separations from the Church which have taken place in the course of history, we tend to put all the blame on those who separated from the Church. But if we look closely at these historical facts and reflect on them "through a more peaceful investigation, free of anger and extravagant zeal," to use the words of Pius XII, we must confess that we were by no means completely free of blame for these separations. Thus, to give only one example, we must admit that in the sad events of the sixteenth-century Reformation, a large share of the blame for this split in the Christian Church must fall on the lives of many prelates, disgracefully lacking in perfection and Christian virtues, men who were not ashamed to combine their love of renaissance literature with a pagan way of life. And afterward, when sharp disputation was necessary to defend and assert the truth, that rule which charity demands, namely, that we should hate error but love the person who errs, was not observed always and everywhere. These are the wrinkles with which human weakness has somewhat disfigured the beautiful face of Christ's Bride.

Since we are now inspired by a true desire for reconciliation, let us begin our ecumenism properly, not hiding the guilt we had in the separations of the past, but humbly confessing them. Let us begin so great a task in the right way, not acting like the Pharisee in the parable, who claimed to be free of all fault, but striking our breasts in a lowly spirit like the humble publican. This is what our Holy Father Paul VI has already done in a remarkable way in this very room, during the speech with which he opened this second session of the Council. All of you could certainly hear how the Pontiff's voice trembled with high emotion, you could see the feeling which stirred his soul, clear signs of the sincerity with which he spoke.

After these few simple words, may I suggest that there be a statement in which this Sacred Synod, lamenting the separations which have taken place up to the present in the Lord's flock, and following in the footsteps of our Holy Father Paul VI, asks pardon of our separated brethren, should they think that they have been injured by sons of the Church, and at the same time testifies that the Church, always a loving mother, completely forgives any injuries she may have received, and forgives in a spirit of love.

STEPHEN A. LEVEN

Auxiliary Bishop of San Antonio,
United States

3
Dangers
of Ecumenism?

I wish to speak about the principles and practice of ecumenism.

Every day it becomes more clear that we need the dialogue, not only with Protestants but also among us bishops.

For there are some Fathers who have already spoken to us frequently in the Council who speak as if the only text in the Holy Bible were St. Matthew 16:18, "Thou are Peter and upon this Rock I will build my Church." In every intervention they argue against the collegiality of the bishops. They preach to us and chastise us as if we were against Peter and his successors or as if we desired to steal away the faith of our flocks and to promote indifferentism.

They speak as if our Holy Father John XXIII had never cited in our day the expression of St. Augustine, "They are our brothers; they will not cease to be our brothers until they cease saying 'Our Father'." They speak as if the whole doctrine of the freedom of conscience due every man, so clearly stated in *Pacem in Terris,* were offensive to pious ears.

Again and again in this aula they continue to chastise us as if the prelate who feels compelled by clear evidence to acknowledge the gifts of the Holy Spirit in persons of other ecclesiastical bodies were denying the faith and giving grave scandal to the innocent.

They prefer to blame non-Catholics whom perhaps they have never seen, than to instruct the children in their parishes. Otherwise why are they so afraid that the effects of ecumenism would not be good? Why aren't their people better instructed? Why aren't their people visited in their homes? Why isn't there an active and working Confraternity of Christian Doctrine in their parishes?

It seems the dangers arising from ecumenism may be exaggerated. The prelates who seek a sincere and fruitful dialogue with non-Catholics are not the ones who show disaffection and disloyalty to the Holy Father. It is not our people who miss Mass on Sunday, refuse the sacraments and vote the Communist ticket.

It is not we who make little of the well-known and often repeated (by word and example) desire of Pope Paul VI and John XXIII. And what of the will of God who, as St. Paul says (1 Tim. 2:4), "wishes all men to be saved and to come to the knowledge of the truth"? Jesus said (Mark 9:40): "He who is not against you is with you."

Our Catholics are good Catholics, loyal to us bishops, to Holy Mother Church and to the Holy

Father. We have not lost the working class. They are the foundation and the support of the Church.

Venerable conciliar brothers, I pray you: let us put an end to the scandal of mutual recrimination. Let us proceed in an orderly way with the examination and study of this providential movement called ecumenism so that with patience and humility we may achieve that unity for which the Lord Christ prayed at the Last Supper. St. Paul wrote (1 Cor. 13:13): "So there abide faith, hope and charity, there are three; but the greatest of these is charity."

CASIMIR MORCILLO

Archbishop of Saragossa,
Spain

4

Dialogue
Is Possible

1. It is with real joy that we greet this subject of ecumenism which has been put on the agenda of Vatican II. This is the first time that such a matter has been discussed in an ecumenical council.

This does not mean that the Church has passed over her duty of faithfully preserving that essential unity which she entrusts every day to the hands of her Spouse whom she prays to "graciously strengthen her unity"; nor does it mean that she has neglected that maternal care which impels her to open her arms to all those separated from her. The liturgical prayers of Good Friday bear witness to this concern.

But we introduce the subject because, living as we do in "the century of the Church", when Vatican II is working toward a thorough description of the Church, we could not fail to speak of a really important aspect of her proper nature, one which touches on that dynamic movement toward church unity which we call ecumenism.

2. There is another remarkable aspect of the schema. That is *its positive tone,* so that many of the warnings and all the condemnations which we used to read in previous texts have disappeared. What has happened? The Church was not ignorant of the Christian elements contained in the separated denominations. They come from her own bosom; they preserve "traces of the Church"; they contain nuggets of gold reminding us of the vein from which they have been mined. But the Church was shying away from the dangers of religion without dogmas, of indifference, and of pan-Christianity, dangers which had to be guarded against at the beginning of the ecumenical movement.

It seems that these dangers are now diminished or have almost completely disappeared. And the Church, who has always deeply lamented division, praises the desires of our separated brothers to work against this division.

The positive aspect of this decree fits in extraordinarily well with the direction of the Council. The contemporary ecumenical effort has many of those virtues best suited for achieving this goal which we share "that all may be one". Would it not be out of place in trying to solve this great problem, to refuse the cooperation offered by our separated brothers?

3. It is a great achievement that this subject has been brought forward in the Council and that its tone is so positive. But is it possible for us to make progress in the methods we employ?

We know that our separated brothers completely reject the invitation to "return". They do not see themselves as responsible for the division, they believe that they belong to the Church of Christ and have preserved the central core of Christianity with complete fidelity. The idea of "return" is intolerable to them and dries up at the roots any possibility of working together.

On the other hand it is true that the Church, aware of her unity and truth, cannot be unfaithful to her own office, which is to be the "pillar and foundation of truth". The better-informed among our separated brothers know what Catholic dogma teaches. Although it seems hard to them, they are sure that they will come up against this fact in the ecumenical movement and they are not annoyed when we recall it. On the contrary, they ask us not to hide anything out of politeness or a desire to avoid raising the problems of division in an unpleasant way.

But there is a further question at this moment of the Council which is preparing the way for unity: *Is it possible to carry on a real dialogue* in which the participants are faithful to what they believe, yet progress is made toward the truth, without the whole enterprise being condemned to fruitlessness ahead of time by an *a priori* No?

I believe that real dialogue is possible without betraying dogma or giving a detailed explanation of all doctrine. I am even convinced that the Second Vatican Council, in conformity with its constitution, should, if possible, undertake this task. We are not trying here to outline the fundamental principles of some methodology but I suspect that such a methodology would respect two realities: (1) the truth, first of all, which does not belong to us, but to Christ, the Gospel, the Church; (2) secondly, a profound reverence for our partner in the dialogue, who without protest accepts our presence with our complete Catholic dogma; we then in turn are bound to acknowledge our brother's sincere understanding of the nature of the Church.

Once these fraternal relations have been acknowledged, which are something different from dogmas, a more complete knowledge can develop in the course of time, along with the elimination of prejudice and closer collaboration.

Finally, we are not going into particular issues; all we say is that such a method is possible. St. Thomas, who is in favor of moving from a position shared in common to a further, more perfect position, has no objection to our procedure. The Sovereign Pontiffs favor such a procedure both by their example in our day and by their teaching at an earlier period on the *"vestigia"* or "traces" of the Church.

The further judgment which will be passed on this schema depends on the attitude toward the method of ecumenism. That is why the following question is of the highest importance: It is possible to engage with our separated brothers in sincere dialogue which will help the ecumenical efforts of Christianity? How far should we go, and how should we conduct ourselves?

Perhaps the Council prefers to make a start and patiently look for the right opportunity.

But meanwhile—and this is my proposal—I suggest:

1. That a preface begin by expressing the intention of drawing up a decree which takes all the present circumstances into consideration and leaves the way open for future developments.

2. That concern for method be strengthened, and that this concern take the form of practical principles of procedure.

3. That the title of the schema be changed so that where it now reads "Principles of Catholic Ecumenism" it will read "Catholic Principles of Ecumenism". My reasons for this suggestion are as follows:

(a) It is easier to test the true elements of the ecumenical movement from our Catholic principles than to work out some new Catholic ecumenism from scratch.

(b) It creates less of a problem of terminology if we keep the normal notion of ecumenism which is found in the documents of the Church's teaching authority.

(c) It is more in keeping with the nature of the Council, which, as far as possible, agrees with the good things which already exist and tries to strengthen them. But if we were to propose a Catholic ecumenism this would give the appearance of trying to completely discourage the "ecumenical movement"; of overlooking faculties of ecumenism, which have not yet been adequately studied and developed; of creating the appearance of two ecumenisms, instead of strengthening what is there by harmonious cooperation.

JOHN CARMEL HEENAN

Archbishop of Westminster,
England

5

Ecumenism in
England

The Hierarchy of England and Wales gives its
ready approval to the Constitution *"De Oecu-
menismo"* which it receives with joy. I say "with
joy" because the document shows us the mind of
the Church and gives guidance for the future. We
have all awaited this guidance from the supreme
authority of the Church. Without it our ecumenical work cannot make progress.

There are those who have thought that the
Catholics of England are indifferent to the ecumenical movement. Indeed some of our separated brethren in England have turned to Catholics outside our country in search of ecumenical
dialogue. We obviously have no wish in any way
to restrict their freedom to attend international
ecumenical gatherings in any part of the world.
We do feel, however, that it is of the greatest importance for this Council to recommend that normally, and as a general rule, the dialogue between
Catholics and other Christians should take place

in the country where they live. It should recommend, moreover, that so far as the Catholic side is concerned, the dialogue should come under the authority of the local hierarchy.

We have two reasons for our proposals:

(a) It is fitting for the dialogue to be held against the background of those local conditions under which the Catholics and other Christians concerned live at home.

(b) If eventually unity is reached, all these Christians will have to learn to live with each other.

For our part we promise our separated brethren that we shall cordially promote the ecumenical dialogue in England and Wales.

Gladly we proclaim our belief in the help and inspiration toward visible union given by the Holy Spirit to all Christians of goodwill. Without God's help ecumenical activity could not have started, nor could it continue. The Holy Spirit, and, indeed, Christian good sense assure us that all who rejoice in the name of Christ (if I may use the words of Pope John) should be united amongst themselves. They should have regard for the greatness of our common heritage and should forget past injuries. Thus charity may be in control and the spirit of dissension cast out. This union is more than ever necessary today since so many enemies of Christ are now seeking to destroy his kingdom.

At the beginning of the second session, Pope Paul declared that everyone, Catholics and separated brethren alike, should sincerely seek unity with humble and contrite heart. The document rightly says that the first step toward union must be a renewal of the spiritual life of the individual. Union will not be achieved through argument: it will be won by virtuous living.

In this spirit of charity and humility, and without in any way wishing to be obstructive, we must frankly outline to the Fathers of the Council a certain difficulty. The nature of ecumenical activity is not yet sufficiently clear and its objectives have not yet been fully explored. It is necessary for our aims and motives in the ecumenical dialogue to be made plain to all. Both the immediate and the ultimate objectives must be quite definitely stated.

Let me speak first of the immediate objective. The ecumenical dialogue is not undertaken with individual souls in mind, nor in order to gain the better of an argument. The dialogue has to be a sincere attempt to understand the beliefs of our separated brethren. It must also present and explain Catholic teaching to them. It is a coming together of brothers not an encounter of enemies. It takes place mainly between communities, that is, between the Catholic Church and non-Catholic Christian churches or communities. It is rooted in mutual trust and complete charity. On neither side is it an attempt to win an argument.

The final aim of ecumenical activity is, of course, the visible union of all Christians in the one Church of Christ. The immediate objective, however, is mutual understanding and love amongst those who are united by baptism but divided by doctrine. At the moment we must work for the first objective—the ultimate aim is not within our power.

It is right to praise the ecumenical dialogue. It seems to us, however, that we should also take note of our obligation to preach the whole truth to all men. That obligation arises from Christ's command to his Apostles and it must be carried out firmly, gently and with great humility by those to whom by God's grace the fullness of Christ's teaching has been given.

We should therefore like this document clearly to state *both* the necessity of the ecumenical dialogue *and* the obligation, imposed by Christ, of preaching the whole truth. Our separated brethren will not resent such preaching, for it comes from a good and honest conscience and shows our desire to follow Christ's command. In this way the demands of both charity and Christian truth are satisfied. If such a declaration were added to this document, the whole cause of ecumenism would be helped. For there are Catholics who are doubtful about all this ecumenical activity. They wonder if any good will come of it. They are greatly concerned about the dangers arising from ecumenism. They are willing enough to co-operate with other Christians in the social field and to combine with them in works of charity. But, as we know, this is simply not good enough. The renewal of the Church requires a true religious dialogue. The Chief Shepherd calls for this; the Church herself desires it.

Christians living in England can still remember the days when bitter strife divided them, and when social life was soured by acrimony. Catholics and

Protestants both regarded themselves as being in a state of war and sought each other's defeat. We give heartfelt thanks to God for the friendship and goodwill now flourishing between Christians. In the name of the whole hierarchy of England and Wales, we readily declare our intention of doing everything, short of denying our faith, to bring about the union of Christians. We wish to undertake a fuller and more frequent dialogue with all Christians, of whatever denomination.

At the Last Supper, in the final hours of his life on earth, Christ prayed to the Father that all his disciples should be one. The prayer of Christ cannot be in vain. Let all, therefore, both the Catholics and the separated brethren, so dear to us, strive that under the protection of Mary the Mother of God, the coming of the kingdom of Christ in the unity of the Church may soon be brought nearer.

6

Clarifications

The Secretariat for Promoting the Union of Christians accepts with great gratitude all the amendments or clarifications suggested for the first three chapters of the schema. Perhaps it would be useful to comment at greater length on some of the things which have been said.

In the discussion there was frequent mention of the dangers which the ecumenical movement might create: indifferentism, interdenominationalism, false irenicism, doubts about faith and so forth. It is certainly true that these dangers are present when, as sometimes happens, men who may mean well, but lack caution and prudence, speak or write about the problem of union. But the remedy for this danger is not to give up action to promote unity, but instead for Sacred Pastors to watch over it properly, direct it, and where necessary, intelligently to correct it. I say that Sacred Pastors should do this, for the task of promoting union is principally the responsibility of the local Ordinary, just as the general responsibility for preaching the Gospel and shepherding

the flock of Christ is his. Certain principles and
general laws for promoting Christian unity can be
drawn up, compiled and more fully explained in
an "Ecumenical Directory" by the Holy See and
the Unity Secretariat, acting in the name of the
Holy See, but it will be up to the bishops to apply
and adapt these laws. For it is obvious that the
religious situation varies enormously in different
parts of the world, just as the way of acting of our
non-Catholic Christian brothers varies in different
regions of the world. Only those who live there
can know these circumstances completely and
form an adequate judgment. Therefore it will be
extremely useful if a regional Secretariat is set
up by bishops' conferences in different regions to
work together with the Roman Secretariat and the
bishops of the region in showing concern for all
ecumenical work, watching over it and promoting it.

In this way the danger of *a kind of false ecumenism,* which some fear, will also be avoided,
and provision will be made that only those will
carry on theological conversations who "by their
knowledge of theology and firm adherence to the
principles and norms established by the Church
in this matter have shown themselves really fitted
for the task" (Instruction of the Holy Office, December 20, 1949, *A.A.S.* 42, 1950, 145). Now the
local Ordinary can know much better than any
branch of the Roman Curia who has these quali-
fications. And if conversations are worked out
in this way there is absolutely no danger of indifferentism, since the very reason for them is to
know clearly *what* teaching should be accepted.

Our Christian brothers have no desire at all that we propose Catholic teaching to them in an incomplete and watered-down form; they want us to tell them clearly what the Catholic Church believes and teaches. Besides, there is nothing so far removed from true ecumenism as a false irenicism which would endanger the purity of Catholic teaching or obscure its true meaning. Conversations of this kind should take place under the watchful care of superiors. It is also the duty of the same superiors to see to it that the *simple* faithful who in regions where there are different religions meet non-Catholics every day and converse with them, are fully instructed in their religion, both by catechetical instruction and solid, well-balanced sermons and lectures. If we do this, the ecumenical movement will not only not be harmful to our faithful, but will rather strengthen and advance them in knowledge and love of the faith.

It has been said that the schema makes too much of the good and true things which are found among our non-Catholic brothers, but fails to give an adequate account of Catholic teaching. In this respect it is important to remember that the schema is not written for non-Catholics, but for those who are sons of the Catholic Church. It presupposes that *they*—would that this were always and everywhere true—*know* Catholic teaching about the nature of the Church, the primacy and infallibility, the unity Christ prayed for, etc. Still it would be possible to give a clearer explanation of the significant truths which have great importance in our ecumenical action. But on the other hand most of those who are Catholics do not know what good and beautiful things are found among our non-Catholic brothers. The primary requirement of all ecumenical activity is that we have an accurate knowledge of them, sincere admiration, and genuine Christian love. For this reason the Sovereign Pontiffs, beginning with Leo XIII, have repeatedly shown what "traces of Christ and gifts of the Holy Spirit" are found among our non-Catholic brothers, and this because of their baptism itself and the graces which flow from baptism. Now anyone who assails this way of acting, automatically attacks the Sovereign Pontiffs from Leo XIII to Paul VI.

Finally, some seem to deny that it is right to pray together for the unity of the Church, since everyone has a different concept of this unity. Now the Instruction of the Holy Office which we have already mentioned has no objection to a joint "recitation of the Our Father or some prayer approved by the Catholic Church" (*A.A.S.* 42, 1950, 146, n.V), and rightly so. For everyone begs God for that unity which Christ desired for his Church, and they leave it to God to decide when and how this will be achieved. Of course it is obviously very necessary for the faithful to be prudently prepared by their pastors for such prayers.

My conclusion is that what has been said seems to show how important it is for all Catholics to have a correct understanding of the ecumenical movement, which the Sovereign Pontiffs desire and promote ever more enthusiastically, but also how prudently and carefully the work must be done, and how it must be made a matter of concern, watchful care, guidance and encouragement by bishops. Furthermore, we should not forget that ecumenical activity, if properly conducted, also does a great deal of good for the faithful. It challenges them to a renewal of their religious and moral life, to a deeper knowledge of Catholic teaching, to the practice of largehearted love. Besides, Christ the Lord surely has richer graces in store for those who work together constantly to fulfill more completely his burning desire "that all may be one".

CARDINAL RAUL SILVA HENRIQUEZ

Archbishop of Santiago,
Chile

7
The
Ecumenical Mentality

The question of how to practice ecumenism is
extremely important for pastoral activity. For it
is not enough to carry on a good argument about
ecumenism and lay down the principles in themselves; we must also *act* ecumenically!

Ecumenism is not a doctrinal affair but rather
a pastoral method in accordance with a particular
"mentality". It is so much the sign of our times
that in our day pastoral activity which is not carried on with an ecumenical mentality becomes by
that very fact an anachronism.

I would like to present for your consideration
two suggestions about the practice of ecumenism.

(1) How to make a beginning.

(2) Its analogical aspect.

1. *How to take the first step in the practice of
ecumenism.*

The recommendation has been made that ecumenism be practiced in order to have brotherly
contact and conversation with our separated

170

brothers "doing the truth in love" (Eph. 4:15).
This text of St. Paul is indeed beautiful, but, Venerable Fathers, we have heard in this Council hall
different ways of interpreting such a statement.
Some begin from the truth and say that ecumenism cannot be practiced properly unless its very
first point of departure is the truth itself, possessed in a static way, clearly explained and safely
established. They conclude that even in prayer
we cannot be one in spirit with those brothers who
are separated from us, as if it were impossible for
true faith, true hope and true love to exist outside the visible boundaries of the Roman Catholic
Church. It is certainly the desire and effort of
all of us to arrive at the unity of an ever deeper
truth, but we should never forget the common
sense principle that the level of actual accomplishment is quite distinct from the level of plan
and intention, so that what comes first when we
want and plan something really comes last on the
level of actual accomplishment.

There are those, on the other hand, who begin
instead from love, and seek unity in truth as the
final goal of their practice of ecumenism. They
begin from love of God and neighbor, so that
under the guidance of the Holy Spirit they may
arrive at the unity of truth.

The proper practice of ecumenism is undoubtedly based on the second of these approaches: it begins from love, which is the
disposition suited by nature to prepare the way
for revealed truth; where the same love is present
it is easier to arrive at the same faith.

Nevertheless, Venerable Fathers, the step

which comes first is not love or charity in itself, but something more concrete and more suited to establish contact.

In the actual practice of human education the step which comes first is neither the possession nor the explanation of a certain truth nor love in general but a warm familiarity with the person to be educated.

St. John Bosco, who made excellent use of the method of love used to say that in this matter love is not enough *("non basta amare")*, but it is necessary for the love itself to manifest itself in some concrete and tangible way and be clearly perceived by the person who is loved.

Besides, is not this the law of incarnation, for the invisible God to become flesh, to actually be heard and seen and touched with the hand?

The first step, therefore, in the practice of ecumenism is not to defend or explain the truth, but to show true love. This love, I repeat, must be shown. There must be a visible and tangible practice of love.

The contents of this chapter *on the practice of ecumenism* then, are extremely important, because they give an explicit indication of some ways that this first step may be concretely initiated.

2. *The analogical aspect of the practice of ecumenism.*

We should keep clearly in mind that the practice of ecumenism is not univocal but analogous. The principle of analogy is of the highest importance not only in theory but also in practice; without analogy theology becomes impossible and pastoral activity is not carried on intelligently.

The other day Cardinal Bea spoke very well about this analogy of the practice of ecumenism. The bishop who introduced the schema had already said that ecumenical activity should be practiced differently according to the demands which different conditions in different countries require.

One of the Fathers has already spoken of the different "types" of separated brothers in the sixteenth and twentieth centuries. So I would like to say something not just about the difference between different centuries in history but also about different geographical regions.

Contemporary European Protestantism, for instance, is basically different from the contemporary Protestantism which is steadily growing in Latin America. Here in Europe we find the sad consequences of a religious struggle which grew out of the faults and sins of Christians in earlier centuries. In Latin America, on the other hand, we are faced with something new springing from many causes, not the least important of which is the movement to meet the religious needs of the masses. For them our pastoral structures are often inadequate, either because of lack of priests, or neglect of the laity, or an incomprehensible liturgy, or catechetical instruction which is heavily moralistic and devotional, or the social injustice of some rich Catholics, or because of a pastoral program geared to a "Christian society" as they say, instead of to a missionary situation, or for other reasons.

There are two things, then, which I believe should be said:

(a) There should be an explicit statement that bishops and bishops' conferences of particular regions should reflect on their own individual problems in different areas and issue appropriate rules of action for them.

(b) There should be a clear statement of the need of a suitable pastoral renewal which steadily gives more attention to the missionary situation than to "Christian society".

The pilgrim Church is an historical reality and its pastoral structures should never be thought of as changeless.

PAUL GOUYON

Coadjutor Archbishop of Rennes,
France

8

No Oversimplification

Now that we have heard about what we have in common with the venerable Churches of the Orthodox East, we must necessarily speak also of those Christian communities which have come into existence in recent centuries. For if we were to say nothing about them, it would seem to be inexplicable neglect, or even perhaps a sign of less affection, since true love always is concerned to forget no one who is really loved. So I am very happy that we are considering those communities which are linked to us by cherished and holy bonds, by the very name of Jesus Christ and by the sacrament of baptism. It is a source of joy to us that the faithful of these communities are called *our real brothers,* who can live in the love of Christ and be raised up by supernatural gifts. I would like to offer what I have to say as a sign of respect for those beloved observers who attend our discussions every day in such a friendly and tactful way.

However, to give to our work all the ecumenical value which men expect from it, I ask that as far as possible, nothing be left out, nothing be confused, nothing be oversimplified.

1. *We should not forget anything which deserves to be remembered.* We obviously want to refer to all those large communities in which men today gather together, which acknowledge Christ as Lord and Savior. But we look in vain for any clear allusion to the great Anglican community, which in its origins is certainly quite distinct and different from the communities of the Reformation. I would like to see explicit mention of this community.

Besides, the word "community" suggests a meaning which belongs almost exclusively to sociology or the non-religious world. Would it not be possible for us to find another term in Sacred Scripture or in Tradition which would be more in conformity with the religious character of these communities. I would suggest the word "communion" (*koinonia*) which, furthermore, is fully in accord with Church tradition.

2. *Nothing should be confused, but instead those things which are different should be clearly distinguished from one another.*

It is rather unusual that the Orthodox Churches should be dealt with along with the communities of which we have just spoken. It would satisfy me better if there were different and separate chapters for the Orthodox Churches, for the Anglican communion and for the communions which grew out of the Reformation. It would be good to take account of the distinct personality of each community.

Where the text approved at New Delhi by the World Council of Churches is cited, I would like to take this opportunity to show our respect for that extraordinary ecumenical organization and to express our joy for the remarkable work it is carrying on, unquestionably guided by the inspiration of the Holy Spirit. However, I should like to point out that such a text should not be presented as a formal creed, since in the minds of its authors it is nothing more than a "basis of union" for those Churches and communities which belong to the World Council of Churches. At the same time we must not forget that the World Council of Churches also includes the venerable Orthodox Churches and it would therefore be better if its statements were not attributed only to the Churches of the Reformation. I would be happy to see this text published with explicit mention of the great work which has already been accomplished by this World Council of Churches up to the present.

3. *Nothing essential should be oversimplified.* It is said that the denominations which have grown out of the Reformation, in their desire to emphasize the transcendence of God, have come to deny the essential mediation of the Church. By saying that, we attribute to them an opinion which they do not hold. There are also other opinions attributed to them which they do not hold. Even the famous dictum *"Soli Deo gloria, sola Scriptura, sola fide"* ("To God alone be glory, by scripture alone, by faith alone") does not ade-

quately express what they think. The causes of
the Reformation cannot be explained in terms of
doctrine alone; there are other causes as well,
which have nothing to do with theology.

It is very good to remember that the goal set
up by the Secretariat for Unity excludes everything which would imply that a separation exists
between us and other Christians on the deepest
level. We should rejoice that the spirit of love is
replacing attempts at apologetics which, while not
altogether useless, were also the source of fruitless
quarrels. Truth itself demands that we at least
carefully state what we have in common so that
we may experience compunction for our division
and desire and seriously strive to fulfill the last
prayer of Christ Our Lord "That they may be
one". This could be the theme of a practical directory of ecumenism.

In any case, we are now more certain that
mutual dialogue and prayer have become possible. Because of this certainty it also becomes possible for us to carry on together a deeper study
of our faith in Jesus Christ, and of his manifestation to the whole world. The immeasurable
achievement of this Vatican Council will be the
fruitful help it has given us in this matter.

SERGIO MENDEZ ARCEO

Bishop of Cuernavaca,
Mexico

9

The Church, an Open Community

"Praise be to the God and Father of our Lord Jesus Christ, who has bestowed on us in Christ every spiritual blessing in the heavenly realms" (Eph. 1:3), for among the good things which we bishops gathered together in Council experience, the movement we call ecumenism has the place of honor. It is the rich fruit of faith, hope, charity, humility, compunction and sincerity and the road which leads us to that fullness of unity in truth to which the Spirit of truth is leading all of us (John 16:13).

I find the decree eminently acceptable, but we must remember that this is the first time the Catholic Church has systematically and solemnly defined its ecumenism for our brothers in Christ who are not Catholics and for the whole world, both of whom eagerly look forward to what we have to say. I have experienced the good results of ecumenism for some time now. Last year in the Council hall I expressed my hopes for its future success. Now, in a spirit of joy, let me humbly indicate a few points of possible improvement in the decree so skillfully prepared for the salvation of souls by the Unity Secretariat.

1. The organized communities which can be called Churches or ecclesial communities are considered, but nothing has been said about other communities, which can better be conceived as movements. The Pentecostals, for instance, have an extraordinary vitality, are filled with active love, possess a well-adapted form of worship, and are sociologically almost perfect. They are usually aggressive and sustained more by feelings than by faith. But they cannot be overlooked, and our other brothers throughout America (North, Central, South and the Islands) are studying them very closely. I have no solutions, but I raise the question.

2. I believe it is not only desirable but absolutely necessary to put stronger emphasis on the very special part which practical pastoral implementation of the liturgical and biblical movements can play in the work of promoting unity with our brothers who are not Catholics.

The significance of worship centered around Christ and the Scriptures is abundantly clear to everyone, for both pertain to the essence of any genuine Christianity.

The great value given to the Scriptures by our brothers who are not Catholics, their diligent use of them and the spiritual profit they derive from them are given high praise. But there is no mention of their liturgical renewal, which comes from the liturgical renewal of the Catholic Church and joins all of us Christians together in a fruitful and intimate union.

Since experience means so much in pastoral matters, I propose these two suggestions:

(a) Ecumenism has its roots in the work of Newman and the Tractarians, who among other things, made a great deal of the liturgy. Another fact worth recalling is that when Lambert Beauduin, to whom so much credit is due as the father of pastoral liturgy, was in Sofia, he started Angelo Roncalli thinking about the importance of the ecumenical movement.

(b) May I mention in this Council hall that in my diocese I undertook a liturgical and biblical renovation of the Cathedral and its public worship. Then, without me doing anything special to promote ecumenism, our brothers who are not Catholics came to me and now I converse with them in friendship and love.

3. Last year when I spoke with a certain timidity and reserve about a condemnation of antisemitism I had a sure hope that this matter would some day be dealt with, as we now see that it is. The question about the Jews should be dealt with entirely apart from the question of non-Christians because of the especially close bond which unites us to the Jews, and which is recognized in the document. There is another bond which should not be omitted: God's choice of this people, still in force, which St. Paul so strongly emphasizes.

The Jews, then, should by no means be excluded from our consideration, so that Catholic ecumenism may be enriched. Besides, this will certainly not be offensive to our other brothers,

since it highlights what we have in common: the
Scriptures and the history of salvation in its past,
present, and eschatological stages.

4. Our consideration should take religious
liberty as its starting point if it is to have a true
perspective, for religious liberty is not a corollary,
or an appendix, or a concession to the modern
mood, but a fundamental and eminently Catholic
principle.

A vision of progressive relationships in logical
order would include: the Church of Christ and
the atheistic world, the Church and religious men
without formal religious affiliation, the Church
and non-Christian religions, the Church and Is-
lam, the Church and all Christians.

Progress, therefore must be made by stages
toward unity, for if we were to make unity our
starting point it would be difficult to avoid intolerance. Besides, unity without freedom is not religious unity.

The Church should be clearly presented as the
sacrament of unity in the world as the Eucharist
is the sacrament of unity in the Church.

For the true Church of Christ is the leaven of
unity in the world even though not everyone is
gathered together in her, even though because of
the so-called population explosion it may seem to
be and remain a tiny flock. The Church as the
sacrament of unity is the means of achieving unity.

And do not say that this is no longer Christian
ecumenism. The goal of ecumenism is, by the
witness of our own faith, to seek unity with those
who give us a witness to their own religion. It is a

unity of hearts which is to lead to a unity of minds in the whole world.

Furthermore, the method is always the same, to clear away the human structures so that we may practice the Gospel of Christ as fully as possible and offer it to others.

5. It seems that the section on the Jews and religious liberty should not be omitted. Another question which is most appropriate concerns men of many religions joined together in an organization whose origins, as we know from history, are completely Christian, which still remains partially Christian, and is now renewing its Christian character. We should undertake a reappraisal of the penalties decreed by the Church at various times against this group, lest both good and bad be cut off from the Church, contrary to the Lord's teaching that the weeds should be left so as not to root up the wheat at the same time. I am speaking of the Freemasons. Not a few of them are anti-Christian, but very many of them believe in a God who reveals himself, and bear the Christian name, or at least do not plot against the Church or civil authority. There are those among them who want the Church to speak to them.

Venerable Fathers: ecumenism is really a new movement, and stands out as the principal feature of the *aggiornamento* set on foot by the saintly John XXIII, who was so intimately and so obviously led by the Holy Spirit. Paul VI, the head of the College of bishops, the rock on which the Church is founded, continues indefatigably to carry on the heritage of John XXIII with the efficiency and order which are his.

We are now offered the opportunity to remedy our past lack of the ecumenical spirit, a fault which we can never adequately lament. Let us all strive with all our energies, with a heart of flesh (Ez. 36:26), made new in mind (Eph. 4:23) to promulgate this decree to mankind as soon as possible, a pledge of peace in unity.

GEORGE FLAHIFF

Archbishop of Winnipeg,
Canada

10

Man's Disorder and God's Design

I agree with the numerous cardinals and bishops who have praised the schema on ecumenism because of its historical importance in the life of the Church and the way it strengthens the spread of the Gospel in the world. This schema is in full agreement with what Pope John XXIII and Pope Paul VI have said about the purpose of the Second Vatican Council and I find it eminently satisfactory.

Yet it seems to me that there should be more emphasis on the historical aspect of the unhappy division among Christians. Schisms among Christians should be described dynamically. Is it not also our task to arrive at some understanding of the meaning or significance of divisions in the history of the Church? We all know that schisms among Christians have very unhappy consequences, which weaken the missionary drive of the Church and set up many obstacles to the spread of the Gospel. But since God, the Lord

of all the events of history, has allowed schisms,
we must search out their positive meaning. For
we fully believe that the history of salvation which
begins in Israel and reaches its peak in Jesus
Christ, still continues in the pilgrim Church.

What then does God want to teach us through
schisms?

(a) Schisms among Christians are brought
about as a consequence of sin, sin in which the
whole Christian people shares. Although it is not
for us to put the past on trial, as Pope John XXIII
said, all Christian communities or Churches are
bound to acknowledge their faults. As long as
they last, divisions accuse us before God and pronounce divine judgment upon us sinners. These
terrible schisms should always remind the Church
that she is not yet as holy as she should be and
not yet perfectly obedient to her vocation to be
catholic.

(b) There is another still more positive aspect
of our divisions. Just as God, the Lord of mercy,
who always draws good from evil, graciously extended salvation to the gentiles — as St. Paul
teaches—in a similar way through the division of
the Churches he wants to give many gifts of the
Holy Spirit to his people in the contemporary situation. Is not the ecumenical movement itself the
principal fruit of the Spirit acting in this divided
people? I am fully convinced that the ecumenical
movement is the work of the Holy Spirit through
which out of schisms, or better, out of the effort to
overcome them, all the Churches profit immensely, are challenged to renewal, find new ways of
acting in love, and come to a deeper understand-

ing of the Gospel. In this ecumenical movement, for the first time in history all the Churches and ecclesiastical communities witness together to Jesus the Savior, thus giving new vigor to the proclamation of the Gospel in the world.

This dynamic aspect, which highlights the work of the Holy Spirit, seems more important for an understanding of the ecumenical movement than a listing of the ecclesial values which have been preserved in other communities, which, by the way, is faithfully done in the schema. Through ecumenical activities the Spirit of God himself brings forth the varied fruit he wishes and leads all Christians to greater fidelity to the will of God.

If the historical and dynamic aspect of ecumenism is explained, it will be more evident that what is said about ecumenism is not a definition or final judgment, but instead only the beginning of an action or development whose author is the Spirit of God himself.

ANDREA PANGRAZIO

Archbishop of Gorizia,
Italy

11

The Mystery of the History of the Church

The remarks I wish to make come under three headings: (1) a description of the Catholic Church, (2) a description of non-Catholic communities, (3) a comparison of the Catholic Church and other ecclesial communities.

The description of the Catholic Church is too static and abstract, and the dynamic and concretely historical aspects of the Church are neglected; yet these seem to be extremely important for the ecumenical dialogue. In my opinion, the *mystery of the Church's history* does not get enough attention.

In the history of the people of God in the Old Testament the Church can and should contemplate the mystery of her own history mirrored in a type, as Paul says to the Corinthians. "All these things that happened to them were symbolic, and were recorded for our benefit as a warning. For upon us the fulfillment of the ages has come" (1 Cor. 10:11).

Just as God in his unsearchable justice punished his people of the Old Covenant in their history for their infidelity, and raised them up again in his almighty power, as he saved them and exalted them when they repented and begged for divine mercy, so he does the same thing now for his people gathered together in the Church of the New Covenant.

In the history of the Church, through the work of the Holy Spirit and the cooperation or resistance of men, events often follow one another in a completely unsuspected and unexpected way, so that no theological system can foresee or understand them. For example, which of the great thirteenth-century theologians would have conceived the possibility of that great Western schism which tore the Church into shreds in the sixteenth century, or of the distortions and abuses which defaced the Church in the period before the Reformation? On the other hand, who at the time of the Reformation could have foretold that remarkable strengthening of the Church which God through his grace brought about after the Council of Trent?

It seems to me that these reflections on the mysterious character of the Church's history is of supreme importance for Catholic ecumenism. For just as the people of God in the Old Covenant, knowing by revelation the merciful purpose of God, always could and should have hoped that God, even by unsuspected deeds, would bring good out of the history of this people weighted down with calamity, so in similar fashion the peo-

ple of the New Covenant can and should nourish
the hope that in his gracious mercy and in a way
as yet unknown to us, God will lead his Church
along paths which none of us can foresee or
predict.

In my humble opinion, this aspect of the divine
dynamism which pulses in the history of the
Church should be more clearly emphasized.
Through this dynamic force God can produce
events, developments and changes, not only in
separated communities but also in the Catholic
Church, which our generation and our Council as
well simply cannot foresee.

By such deeds God can make possible that desired union of separate Christianities which today
still seems impossible. This will be possible, however, only if all Christians will be obedient to the
inspirations of divine grace.

My second remark touches on the description
of non-Catholic communities. It is a good thing
to list all those elements of the Church which by
God's grace have been preserved in these communities and continue to produce saving effects.
But to express my honest opinion, it seems to me
that such a catalogue is too "quantitative", if I may
use the expression. It seems that these elements
have simply been piled together. I believe that a
bond is needed to unite these separate elements.

We should point to the *center*, to which all these
elements are related, and without which they cannot be explained. This bond and center is *Christ*
himself, whom all Christians acknowledge as
Lord of the Church, whom the Christians of all
communities unquestionably want to serve faith-

fully, and who graciously accomplishes wonderful things even in separated communities by his active presence through the Holy Spirit, not by any merit of men but by his gracious mercy alone.

A third remark: to arrive at a fair estimate of both the unity which now exists among Christians and the diversity which still remains, it seems very important to me to pay close attention to the *hierarchical order* of revealed truths which express the mystery of Christ and those elements which make up the Church.

Although all the truths revealed by divine faith are to be believed with the same divine faith and all those elements which make up the Church must be kept with equal fidelity, not all of them are of equal importance.

Some truths are *on the level of our final goal,* such as the mystery of the Blessed Trinity, the Incarnation and Redemption, God's love and mercy toward sinful humanity, eternal life in the perfect kingdom of God, and others.

Other truths are *on the level of means toward salvation,* such as that there are seven sacraments, truths concerning the hierarchical structure of the Church, the apostolic succession, and others. These truths concern the means which are given by Christ to the Church for her pilgrim journey here on earth; when this journey comes to an end, so also do these means.

Now doctrinal differences among Christians have less to do with these primary truths on the level of our final goal, and deal mostly with truths on the level of means, which are certainly subordinate to those other primary truths.

But we can say that the unity of Christians consists in a common faith and belief in those truths which concern our final goal.

If we explicitly make these distinctions in conformity with the hierarchy of truths and elements, I think the existing unity among all Christians will be seen more clearly, and it will become evident that all Christians are already a family united in the primary truths of the Christian religion.

JOSEPH TAWIL

Greek-Melchite Patriarchal Vicar
for the Eparchy of Damascus

12

A Voice from the East

There are three comments I would like to submit on the first chapter of the ecumenism schema.

1. Instead of speaking of principles of Catholic ecumenism, it would be better to speak of Catholic principles of ecumenism. If ecumenism really is a movement of all Christians toward a greater unity, it cannot strictly be called Catholic, Orthodox, or Anglican, or by any other such name.

But it is possible to speak of Catholic or Orthodox or Anglican or other principles of the same ecumenism.

2. Divisions are dealt with in a purely descriptive way, but nothing at all is said about the theology itself of division. On this subject the Sacred Scriptures shed some light:

The people of God has unity when, in quest of salvation by faith, it receives the Promise; on the contrary it is divided when, trusting in the flesh, it loses the Promise. This is the consistent theol-

ogy of the books of the Law and the Prophets. It
is found again in the New Covenant in the division
of the main part of Israel, which trusted more in
the Law than in faith. Afterward the Church —
the new people of God—ran after the temptation
to "Judaize", to "Hellenize" (5th century), to
"Latinize" (11th century), and finally to "Ro-
manize" (16th century). Then she found she had
the righteousness of the flesh and no longer that
of faith (Phil. 3:7-9).

But the gifts of God are irrevocable (Rom.
11:29). He never abandons his people, so that if
unity is given by grace, the divisions themselves
are directed to a greater grace, so that we may all
receive mercy. The marvelous works of God from
the Old Covenant to the present are such that the
divisions which grow out of the denial that salvation is a free gift lead to a free gift which is even
more abundant. The Bible's vision of the unity
and division of the people of God puts everything
in the history of the Church in the light of mercy
and grace "for in making all mankind prisoners
to disobedience, God's purpose was to show mercy
to all mankind" (Rom. 11:32).

The Council Fathers, the great majority of
them of the Latin rite, have undoubtedly been surprised that the Eastern Fathers do not always
agree. The first thing to be said is that this division
is not any more unusual than the disagreements of
the Latin Fathers among themselves. It comes
from the following causes:

(1) Positive traditions which are distinct, in-
herited together with the Orthodox—a Byzantine,
a Syrian, or a Coptic tradition, fundamentally

similar to one another yet at the same time noticeably different.

(2) The carry over of different group psychologies which come from the structure of different communities, long before the conversion of the peoples of Central and Western Europe, that is, of the Slavs, the Germans and the English. Consequently there is a separate life for 1,500 years, or 1,300 years, for example, in the case of the Maronites.

(3) The Catholic Easterners are also different according to their different degrees of Latinization; for our Churches are all Latinized. A proof of this is that I have to speak Latin in this Council hall. Neither race nor nation makes one an Easterner, but rather the direct living apostolic tradition, not in contradiction with Latinity, but different from it. Anyone who has simply followed a course of theology remembers that the arguments from tradition are given by citing first the Greek Fathers, then the Latin Fathers, mutually confirming each other by their different origins. From this it is understandable that communities which are strongly Latinized by their history are not so readily sensitive to ecumenical needs, and that one or another of the Fathers, reflecting this mentality, asked for a unified Code within Catholicism for the two Churches of the East and the West, and a single jurisdiction, something inconceivable for anyone who has kept the positive meaning of Orthodox tradition and sensibilities.

In conclusion, remember that all the Catholic Churches of the East taken together represent hardly two per cent of Orthodoxy as a whole, which numbers more than 200,000,000, of which 180,000,000 are of the Byzantine rite, 15,-000,000 of the Coptic and Ethiopian rite and 5,000,000 of the Syrian. Now the only interest these Churches have from an ecumenical viewpoint is in relation to Orthodoxy, whose tradition they are thought to represent. Actually, each of them looks toward its fulfillment, and has no right to consider itself as definitely closed, but is only a stage on the road to unity. Now to ask for a unified Code for the two Churches of the East and West or a unified jurisdiction would be to close all the paths which lead to ecumenism, to enclose oneself in a deadly isolation, and to become for the universal Church a positive obstacle to union.

GERARD HUYGHE

Bishop of Arras,
France

13

We Must All Be Converted

The excellent ecumenism schema says that if Catholics live their own faith more fully, then the approach to this home of the Catholic Church will be more easily open to all men.

It is a source of great joy that the authors of our schema have used the word "approach" preferring it to the word "return". For we must admit that a few years ago many of us in speaking of the unity of Christians used to look to the past and say: "Unity cannot be achieved unless all those who fell into schism or heresy, and thus left the Church at one or another moment in history, return to the Church. They will have to renounce their errors and accept dogmas which they had either rejected or never accepted; let them come back to us, chained hand and foot, and we who glory in the name of Catholic, dispassionately contemplating such a return of those who have been separated, will change nothing in our Catholic Church which is the only true and perfect Church." Such a *return* would be nothing but an *unconditional surrender*.

But today we look at all those things in quite a different way and the words of John XXIII and Paul VI, full of humility, have helped us to do so. For today we speak like this: "It is true that our brothers have left us, but we too have sinned" and as Pope Paul VI has said "We humbly ask pardon of God and pardon from our brothers themselves."

What are the conditions in which this eagerly desired unity can take place? They have already been outlined very well in this Council hall; but I would like strongly to emphasize just two more of them while making a deeper study of the meaning of the word "approach".

These are the two conditions: (1) The conversion of all Christians, (2) The joint action of all Christians.

1. *We must all be converted to Christ together.* The unity we hope for is both gift and promise; if we Catholics were arrogantly to think that unity is some private possession of ours, entrusted to our diligent and heroic care, this would be sheer pride and we would have to be called traitors to unity. This unity has been given to us only so that we may preserve it together with all our baptized brothers, and so that with eyes always on the future, we may all move ahead together. This is exactly what the Sovereign Pontiff said to the Observers: "The best method for us is not to look at the past, but at the present and especially to the future. We prefer to fix our sights not on what has happened but on what is to be done. We turn

our eyes to something new, to something we must
do, to a dream which we must make a reality."
And the Pontiff used the words of St. Paul: "For-
getting what is behind me, and reaching out for
what is ahead, I press toward the goal to win the
prize which is God's call to life above, in Jesus
Christ" (Phil. 3: 13-14).

To progress along this road, we must constantly
be converted to what is better. Without humility
deeply rooted in the hearts of Christians true unity
will never be able to exist. But this presupposes
that each Christian, each Christian community,
examines its own conscience, refraining from all
bitter comparisons or any malicious judgments,
from condemning others because they are not entirely like us.

This presupposes that we completely get rid of
that legalistic spirit which for too long has been
for us a hindrance to a right conscience. This presupposes that we do not demand more from others
than what is in our common Creed. In the First
Council of Jerusalem we hear the Apostle James,
putting aside his notorious severity and speaking
in this manner to the Christians to restore peace
among them: "My judgment is that we should not
trouble those . . . who are turning to God" (Acts
15:19); and then the Apostles unanimously decreed: "It is the decision of the Holy Spirit, and
our decision, to lay no further burden upon you
beyond these essentials" (Acts 15:28). Finally
this presupposes that we have the greatest respect
and esteem for our brothers, and that, to use the
words of Paul VI: "We devote ourselves with
proper reverence to that religious heritage which

we have received from the ancient past and which we all have in common, which our separated brothers have preserved and parts of which they have even refined and improved" (Discourse of September 29, 1963).

2. *All of us must do everything together in the name of Christ.* Actions always precede words and are better than words. This was fully true of Christ because he began to act and to teach. It applies to us too, because the more closely we are joined together in what we do, the easier it will be to find the road which leads to unity. Where then will it be possible to act together as we should?

The first area of common action is *ecumenical prayer*. For many years now separated Christians have prayed together "for the unity which God wants, and which he himself will bring about at the time and through the means which he has ordained." (This is what Pere Couturier used to say.) Who can deny that the concern to achieve unity which is found today in the hearts of the faithful of each community, and the progress which is clearly evident in our schema on ecumenism, are the fruit of prayer? When separated Christians pray together, by that very fact their hearts are transformed for the better and opened wide to their brothers. Prayer together can be called the builder of unity.

The second area is an *ecumenical collection*. I mean that contribution made by all Christians to help the poor throughout the world. This contribution has a biblical foundation and is really a kind of extension of that community of goods which was practiced in the early Church. It is in itself a visible sign and symbol of Christian unity.

The third area is that of *theological reflection on questions which today are extremely important*. One example would be the question of poverty which must be studied by all Christians as one of the most urgent problems of our time. In this matter hardly anything has yet been done, and a study of this subject carried on together by theologians of different communities will be a mutual help toward effective service of the poor.

The fourth area where we can collaborate is in *community pastoral activity*. Even if we pool our resources we are still a minority in the pagan world today, and this will continue to be a more serious problem because of the steadily increasing population growth in those regions where the Gospel has not been spread. Instead of stupid competition we should work together to spread the Gospel of Christ, in complete loyalty to the faith which we ourselves profess.

My conclusion is that if these conditions are fulfilled, the approach of our brothers to this home of the Church will surely be possible. And this will not take place by any sudden and miraculous change but by a steady invisible kind of movement. Perhaps at long last the day will arrive when we will see that there is no longer any obstacle between us and our brothers who were once separated from us.

May I in closing express this wish: that the Secretariat for Promoting Christian Unity will give us a directory as well so that our activity to achieve unity may be made easier.

CARDINAL VALERIAN GRACIAS

Archbishop of Bombay,
India

14
Serving
the Poor Together

My talk is about cooperation with our separated brothers.

1. Our schema shows how important it is for Christians to work together, because this shows forth the sign of Christ, which is unity in love. *This is to me a source of great joy and satisfaction.* But there is not a clear enough statement that the most wide open way to unity is joint action *in the service of the poor*. Theological work is certainly necessary, but working together clears away many obstacles. As early as 1950 the Plenary Council of India issued the following decree: "Praise is due to those of the faithful who, while observing proper caution and observing the regulations of the Church, work together also with sincere men who are not Catholics to promote the public, social, and moral welfare in conformity with the norms of the natural law." In this social action, at least we can unite without theological bitter-

ness; otherwise, as the English proverb has it, "In the face of a common enemy, if we do not hang together, we shall hang separately." The common enemy, especially in the East, is the well-nigh universal phenomenon of poverty and misery. Once when I was giving a public talk at a meeting in a certain part of India, the chairman of the gathering, a bishop of the Mar Thomites group, remarked, "The world is too strong for a divided Christianity." I have never forgotten those words.

2. It is a sad fact that the invitations of the Sovereign Pontiff (Pius XII) to work together in social and international activity have not had a greater impact on Christians. Paul VI himself, while still archbishop of Milan, said: "The poor are the image of Christ; they are even a living sacrament" (Lenten Pastoral, 1963). Let me remind you of some facts, facts which are indeed grim. I quote from a recent publication *(Christian Responsibility and World Poverty)* to which Cardinal Suenens, Archbishop Heenan, Msgr. Ligutti, Fr. de Lestapis and others have contributed: "In the underdeveloped countries, 150,000,000 families are living in sub-human conditions; two thirds of the population of the world are not receiving the 2,500 calories daily, considered to be a vital minimum; infant mortality still stands at 185 per 1,000 in India and the expectation of life of the new-born is only 32 years in India. The nineteen richest countries representing together only 16% of the world's population control 75% of the world's income. In the underdeveloped countries 150,000,000 families are living under sub-human conditions and 30,000,000 in countries

called prosperous. India has an illiteracy percentage of 83.4%."

And it seems to me that perhaps we do not think enough about the promise we made last year in the message of the Council Fathers to all mankind.

Should we not then present a petition to the Holy Father (through the Council of the Presidency and group of Moderators, etc.) that in the next session priority be given to extended examination of the *seventeenth schema*. For us in Asia and Africa or in South America this is very important.

3. May I add that the discussion of the seventeenth schema has an important connection with the Eucharistic Congress. It will be a preparation for those matters which we shall deal with in the Congress. In most of Asia this Jesus, who for us became needy and who invites us to follow him, has not yet been made known. Therefore we want to have during the Congress a special study, a seminar which will deal with the subject of "food and health", and we hope to have the collaboration of international organizations (such as FAO, Misereor, NCWC, OXFAM, etc.) and national organizations as well.

Bishops and specialists in those needs of our times which disturb our world—hunger, an unjust distribution of wealth, war and peace—will gather in Asia to examine social doctrine so that what the Fathers announced to the world at the beginning of the Council may be more clearly announced to the world. Thus we will better understand what all Christians (Catholics and separated brothers) must do to give the contemporary world a sign of that love which is signified by the Eucharist.

Thus the celebration of the mysteries of the Eucharist will not be a manifestation of glory or propaganda (at least not in our case) but a manifestation of the love of Christ. The Eucharist impels us to show a true witness of poverty and concern for the poor. The image of the Church, as I have already said, is an image of the Church as servant, following the example of her founder who said "I have not come to be served but to serve" and of whom it was said "He went about doing good".

EMILE BLANCHET

Rector of the Institut Catholique
Paris, France

15

No Reunion
Without Theology

Two remarks seem to me to be in order concerning intellectual work which ought to be done, if full preparation is to be made for that union of Christians which we all want, but which cannot be made a reality if each side comes with nothing more than feelings of good will. Such feelings are really necessary, but we are not only concerned with friendly feelings between persons, it is also a matter of truth and conscience which have their own laws.

1. *The importance of this work.*

(a) It is obvious that there is no possibility of true union unless there is sure knowledge of each other's teaching and everything connected with it. Discussion is useful, but only on condition that the participants are not so eager to win that they neglect the first task, which is the need to understand. All these expert theologians, exegetes, historians, psychologists and philosophers who, led only by the love of truth, have carried on what is often a thankless task, have made and continue to make a significant contribution to the union of Christians. To share the same strict methods of scholarship and the same desire of serving the truth alone is in itself a considerable advance, and binds scholars closely together.

A special reason for singling out such work for praise is that in our day there is a temptation to what is sometimes called "activism" as if the only means of actual achievement were the spread of zeal which fixes its attention only on immediate results. But books have their own power, a very great power and—to give a single example—who can say how great was the influence and significance for the issue we are now discussing of Cardinal Newman's book, "An Essay on The Development of Christian Doctrine", an influence which still continues after a hundred years?

But if in something which is so complex, so full of serious difficulties, now and then someone says or writes something which is open to criticism, or not yet mature, or something for which the Christian people are not yet ready, let a warning be given to the degree that the public good demands, but let him be admonished as a son, not as an evil workman who is put permanently under a cloud of suspicion; in this way the spirit of those who devote themselves to such necessary labor will not be broken, which would be harmful to ecumenism.

Furthermore, we should always remember that the religion of our separated brothers cannot be reduced to a series of propositions which can be adequately refuted with good arguments. There is something deeper than these propositions: a vivid grasp of a particular religious reality. In most cases, either in reacting against existing defects or abuses, or because of personal experience, those at the beginning of the separation were men who saw a certain aspect of religious doctrine or Christian life so fully and acutely that they were in danger of neglecting or denying other aspects. Thus the situation became an occasion of error. It is the task of the theologian, with help from a knowledge of psychology, and of the historian who probes below the surface of events, to discover this first vivid intuition from which the rest follows. And this is very important because unless he penetrates to this essential point, he seems to remain on the surface, and leaves his partner in the conversation with the impression that he was not really understood. So the dialogue turns out to be useless.

(2) It is most necessary to give an explanation which makes it clear that if anyone accepts Catholic faith he is not thereby forced to be unfaithful to what he formerly believed, as though he were to reject his own mother. Actually he rejects nothing but negations: he preserves the truths he already believed and expands his vision to other complementary truths, so that what he formerly believed is not destroyed but enriched. What he already possessed is taken up and amplified and finds its place in the Catholic Church where there is the greatest variety of religious families, joined together in the one faith with respect for legitimate diversity. As Pope John XXIII gladly said in speaking of the Council and expressing his

hope for future union, "After the necessary reforms and renewal we must be able to say to those who are still separated from us: 'This beautiful home of the Church is not our possession. If you wish to see and enter, you do not have to come to us: you are in your own home. The house of God is your home'." This is a good example for ecumenical work: the faith has been given to us freely: we do not own it. We are the servants of the truths revealed by God, not its masters. Ecumenical problems, then, must not be oversimplified, since they involve many difficulties and we need to penetrate to the inner living core of the matter. And we should avoid polemics, although the issues are often delicate and a source of concern.

My conclusions are (1) that the importance of the necessary intellectual work should be given greater emphasis and (2) that particular respect should be given not only (as is evident) to the sincerity of those separated from us, but also to the positive elements which they preserve.

EUGENE D'SOUZA

Archbishop of Bhopal,
India

16

Intellectual
Humility

A number of other missionary bishops have endorsed the remarks I am about to make.

We warmly congratulate those who have drawn up the schema for having given us a text which is solid, beautiful, deeply Christian, a text which we hope will definitely fix the new orientation which has taken place in the Church in recent years. I speak of the fact that the Catholic Church as a Church has finally learned humility.

The Sovereign Pontiff himself humbly begged pardon of God and of the separated brothers themselves at the beginning of this session, and the schema urges us to inner renewal and conversion of heart. I want to take a closer look at this last point.

We confess that in this matter the law of progress has had more influence than the law of continuity. For after the famous confession which Pope Adrian VI ordered his legate in Germany to make at the start of the Reformation, such statements were very rarely made in the succeeding centuries. It is right for the Catholic Church to say that she has received the fullness of truth and of the means of grace, but it seemed that from this the false conclusion was drawn that she was practically guiltless.

Confessions have become more frequent in recent decades. But what was confessed, at least by members of the hierarchy, remained limited— limited to moral life and the practice of Christian virtues. The structures of the Church and the way of presenting doctrine were almost never mentioned.

A few days ago other speakers eloquently demonstrated that, quite apart from the need to show a more attractive "face of the Church" to our separated brothers, there is an urgent need to extend inner renewal to the various structures and methods of governing the Church. And there was no effective refutation of this demonstration. So I will speak only about renewal in presentation of doctrine.

It is altogether certain that only the Catholic Church has integrally preserved the deposit of faith; and in the presence of our separated brothers we humbly bear witness to this fact in the Lord. In no official document, indeed never in the exercise of her ordinary teaching office, has she denied any revealed truth or taught error. But when asked whether she has always kept the proper balance, whether she has explained everything appropriately, whether Catholic theology and spiritual teaching has always given the proper emphasis, an objective observer would have to answer that she has not.

The reasons for this are varied. Unrestrained emotion, for instance, or a subjective approach could confuse the issues. The deposit of faith is so complex that everyone can find something there which suits him, something which he can use, as the psychologists say, to "rationalize" his own individual or national character, his tendencies, even his will to power. He will gladly expound such a point, even if as a prelate or a theologian he has authority, and thus he will put forth a teaching which at the very least is one-sided.

So it is a very good thing, even from this point of view, that the schema urges self-denial and humility, and consequently conversion of mind; for the mind cannot be separated from the heart.

Another source of deviation is argumentative debate with a will to win. In controversy, when one side states a thesis the adversary usually states the antithesis, although often what should be proposed is a synthesis. When a particular truth is denied, Catholic theology usually takes a dogmatic definition as a starting point, often develops it in such a way that it becomes exaggerated, and finally yields a total image which is inadequate. And who will dare to claim that classical Catholic theology (in ecclesiology, Mariology, grace, revelation) has yet freed itself sufficiently from this polemical heritage?

Here too, Brothers, we need humility. Let us with sincere and truthful hearts direct our attention to those complementary truths which, as one

of us has well said, our separated brothers sometimes emphasize better than we do.

I want to insist on this point. Just as love is
not perfect unless it is universal and total, so humility too should be total and should include what
I will call intellectual humility, or even doctrinal
humility.

In recent days we have often heard: "We must
propose the whole of the Catholic truth to our
separated brothers". Pardon me if I admit that I
sometimes seem to read between the lines these
words: "Although we are sinners, we Catholics
possess the whole truth; and this is our great
superiority."

It is true that we Catholics need not cultivate
an inferiority complex. But the time is long over-
due for us to get rid of any superiority complex.
And we must certainly do our best to root out
that oversimplification: "We possess the truth;
the others say the same thing as we do or they are
in error; therefore we need not listen to them except to refute them."

Horace said: "To learn from the enemy is legitimate"—a fortiori from brothers in Christ. For
"catholic" means "universal". Just as Christ took
to himself everything human, sin alone excepted,
so Catholicism which is true to its name should
take to itself everything which is Christian, leaving out negations. In actual fact, for the principal
first fruits of renewal we are heavily indebted to
others—for the biblical movement to the Protestants and for the liturgical movement to the Orthodox. Relying on their help, let us abandon those
traditions which belong only to a particular school

of theology or national character or religious order and which we have repeatedly confused with Tradition with a capital "T". Or let us make certain superficial and peripheral devotions give way to what is deep and central. All this can help us to grasp more perfectly the mystery of Christ and the Church.

In this way ecumenism will contribute to the doctrinal *aggiornamento* of the Church. Obviously it is not a question of omitting or watering down certain dogmas out of opportunism or false irenicism. But the questions which are put to us will make us more alert to the full implications of the synthesis we seek. This will be true if we know how to listen with sincerity of heart, to "listen to one another" in the full sense, as the Sovereign Pontiff said in his talk to the Observers. But this presupposes that we are "not self-complacent, but humble-minded" (Rom. 12:16).

Venerable Brothers, successors of the Apostles, let us often meditate on these words of the Apostle: "God forbid that I should boast of anything but the cross of our Lord Jesus Christ" (Gal. 6:14); or these others: "If I am to boast . . . I delight to boast of the weaknesses which humiliate me, and then the power of Christ will come and rest upon me" (2 Cor. 12: 1-9).

LEON ARTHUR ELCHINGER

Coadjutor Archbishop of Strasbourg,
France

17

No Fear of
the Truth

This decree on ecumenism is a gracious gift of God to these our times. All that has been said and done over the years to promote the unity of the Church, and especially the often laborious efforts of the forerunners of Catholic ecumenism, seems to come to fulfillment in this decree. As a certain Council expert (Pere Yves Congar, O.P.) has written, in the service of truth there are certain deeds or events in the Church which are more efficacious than mere statements of doctrine. We can say that this schema is such a deed.

But this holy idea of ecumenism is so important that we should all work to make the schema even better. In studying this schema it occurred to me, a coadjutor bishop in whose territory a third of the Protestant Christians of France live, that a really fundamental condition of the progress and, with God's grace, the success of ecumenism is a sincere and deep reformation of the way we investigate and serve revelation or truth in the Church.

I wish to suggest four reflections to you, **Venerable Brothers**, about the conditions without which it seems to me that ecumenism will not prosper in our present Roman Catholic Church:

1. *Up to now* we have often not dared to confess historical facts which are less than favorable to the reputation of our Church. *Now* the time has come, as Pope Leo XIII said when he opened the Vatican archives, to admit and confess historical truth, even when it is bitter.

We all certainly believe that the Church is holy, just as we believe it is one, catholic and apostolic. But we also know that God has put his holy gifts in vessels of clay (2 Cor. 4:7), that is in men who are sinners. We no longer refuse to confess our sins, as our Holy Father Pope Paul testified in his address of September 29th, and at the reception for our brothers the Observers on October 17th. And this must be not merely a general confession, but must detail all the particular questions and deeds where we have fallen short in various ways, or where divinely-revealed truth has been honored with warmer fervor by our separated brothers.

Let me give three examples of this.

It is a certain historical truth that at the beginning of our divisions, those who took the initiative had no desire to act primarily and unconditionally against unity, but began by seeing that certain truths were fundamental in divine revelation: for instance, the apostolic rights of the Churches, in the schisms of the eleventh century, or again, in the sixteenth-century Reformation, the dogma of justification by faith in the Lord Jesus our Savior, which had been defined at the

First Council of the Apostles in Jerusalem. On the other side of the ledger, what scholar well-versed in this history of those two periods would dare to doubt or deny that some Christians, perhaps many of them, and even Pastors of our Catholic Church, made light of these truths at that time (though they are certain truths) and sinned in various ways against those who bore witness to these truths?

It is also a certain historical truth that in our times the most enthusiastic and certainly most numerous experts and promotors of the ecumenical movement came from Churches separated from our Church, while on the contrary in our Church the pioneers of the movement often, even more often than not, met with exasperating obstruction. This happened, for instance, to Cardinal Mercier, despite his high rank, in his ecumenical efforts with the holy Anglican, Halifax.

Again, in investigating and explaining the truths of divine revelation contained in the Sacred Scriptures, the teaching authority of the Roman Church is undoubtedly of inestimable help and it is quite necessary for us to rely on its careful concern, its prudence and its wisdom. Nevertheless it is an historical fact that our separated brothers have been shown greater brotherly trust within their Churches than our Catholic exegetes, who, on the contrary, have suffered much from their brothers and even from their Pastors, as, for example, Pere Lagrange of distinguished memory in the *Ecole Biblique* of Jerusalem.

2. *Up to now,* when there were controversies between separated Christians, we frequently used

to reject those teachings which we considered false, as totally false. *Now the time has come* to recognize with greater respect that there is also a partial truth, in fact, often a profound truth, in every doctrine taught by our separated brother, which we should profess along with him.

In a press conference last year at the first session of the Council a certain professor, one of the distinguished Observers (Oscar Cullmann), said that Catholics often do not see in some of the denials or limitations which Protestants make, that there is a positive result, a "focusing of the faith on certain really fundamental truths of divine revelation" such as, for instance, personal responsibility in the assent of faith, or the importance of Sacred Scripture in the divine plan of revelation, or the freedom of the Holy Spirit which produces the freedom of the children of God, etc. The time has come in our conversation with our separated brothers to consider first these positive Christian truths by which and in which they fervently live, so that we ourselves with them may live better and more profoundly by these truths. Then it will be possible with God's grace to bear witness before them to those revealed truths in Catholic tradition which we freely hold and which they in our opinion do not accept or do not sufficiently emphasize.

We should likewise give more respectful, brotherly, and trusting attention, and if possible, collaboration to Christian or scientific works such as, for example, the ecumenical collection for both Catholic and Protestant poor during the annual week of prayer for unity in January.

3. *Up to now* many Catholics, even clerics and Pastors, have held the truth of Revelation in the Church in what I might call a passive or static fashion, and have paid no attention to those doctrinal questions raised by our divisions. *Now the time has come* for all of us, each in his own way constantly to investigate divine truth more deeply and with a living faith.

For the certainty of faith consists in our clinging firmly to the Word of God and divine truth. But as long as we are on pilgrimage the investigation or understanding of that Word of God never comes to an end, though the truths which have already been defined stand firm. Faith seeks understanding. In this investigation, which proceeds from love, under the guidance of the apostolic teaching authority instituted by the Lord Jesus for his Church, and with each one exercising that proper prudence which rejects both presumption and timidity, an exchange in faith with our separated brothers can be extremely profitable both for us and for them. To search for truth together, each one loyal to his own belief and respectful of the freedom of others, is a great work of friendship.

Only through this lively faith in the possession and investigation of divine revelation may we hope eventually, with the help of God's grace, to finally arrive at full unity of faith.

4. *Up to now,* especially in the most recent period of our Latin Church, we have very frequently confused *uniformity,* both in liturgical rites and in theological doctrines which express divine revelation, with *unity* of faith, love, and the

worship of the Christian religion. *Now the time has come,* remembering the teaching of Paul the Apostle that there are varieties of graces (1 Cor. 12: 4-11), to recognize, honor and cultivate the freedom of the children of God in the Church of Christ, whether it be freedom of individual persons or of communities.

In the Council hall, my dear brothers, we have by now often experienced what a great diversity there is among us, not of a language (for the only language has been Latin) but of opinions, of aspirations and desires, and even more profoundly, of theological teachings. And yet we have experienced more than ever the deep unity of our faith, love, and worship of God.

When we come to the differences between us and our separated brothers, differences not of faith in divine revelation, but of legitimate theological doctrines in which this faith is expressed; not in the communion of brotherly love, but in legitimate ecclesiastical structures; not in Baptism and the Eucharist and other sacraments of faith established by the Lord, but in rites and prayers which better promote their piety and the glory of God; they—our separated brothers—have a strict right in the Lord that we, far from ignoring or rejecting these differences, should foster them in a spirit of brotherhood, admiration and harmonious zeal.

Finally, let me answer the objection that such an ecumenism can lead to false irenicism or the error of doctrinal relativism. My answer is that ecumenism, thus understood as resting solidly upon Gospel faith, may perhaps lead to a relativism of words, or even of personal ideas, but definitely not to a relativism of faith in divine revelation and holy truth, which ceaselessly transcend the powers of the human mind.

CARDINAL PAUL-EMILE LEGER

Archbishop of Montreal,
Canada

18

Freedom and Diversity

I have two suggestions which deal with promotion of unity in the area of doctrine.

1. My first suggestion concerns a more accurate presentation of the mark of unity of the Church.

We all know that many Catholics and non-Catholics think the Catholic Church favors too monolithic a unity. And perhaps we could admit, actually, that the Church, especially in recent centuries, has cultivated an exaggerated uniformity in doctrine, in worship and in her general discipline. For frequently we have somewhat neglected certain legitimate demands of freedom and diversity within the bounds of unity.

Now many of the Fathers, especially from mission areas, have justly emphasized the importance for well-ordered missionary work of a strong statement saying that unity in the Church of Christ can never stand in the way of legitimate liberty and diversity. The importance of such a statement for ecumenical activity is clear for all of us to see. For the separated Churches and communities also possess their traditions, their institutions, their spiritual heritage, and they have a legitimate desire to preserve them.

Therefore to avoid all ambiguity about the kind of unity which the Catholic Church seeks, in the theological explanation of the unity intended by Christ we should not fail to explain more fully and clearly how in this concept perfect obedience is compatible with supreme freedom, true unity with great diversity. The Sovereign Pontiff himself praised this diversity in his opening address of this second session.

My second suggestion is that better means be provided for settling doctrinal differences. For doctrinal issues create very great difficulties in ecumenical work. And it would be extremely helpful if, as far as possible, some principle could be laid down in this matter, and if that mentality could be fostered—among Catholics, especially Pastors and theologians—which would make it easier to resolve these apparent oppositions.

We all agree that in examining doctrinal issues together with our brothers, love and truth should never suffer harm. But should we not go beyond that? Should we not say clearly that in the investigation which we conduct together with other brothers, when we are confronted with the inexpressible divine mysteries, we must do the truth not only in love but also in humility?

Our dogmas are the end product of a long process of theological inquiry which, in its methods, often differs from the thought patterns of our separated brothers of the West and the East. The separated brothers too have conducted their own theological investigations. Out of these parallel investigations differences have grown which many consider insuperable. In my opinion, these differences will not be resolved unless the separated brothers and we Catholics study the revelation of Christ together in humility. Unfortunately the Church has known many schisms and heresies during her history. But many of them have been healed, as we see in the Fathers of the Church, not by the exercise of authority but by moving ahead together in faith, in love, and in humility.

In this Council the Church has already frequently chosen to speak of her humble pilgrim state. And the desire the Church has shown to confess her sins is very important. But now the Church, especially in our time, also needs *intellectual humility*. We frequently hear it said that the Catholic possesses the full truth revealed by Christ. This statement can be correctly understood, of course, if the proper distinctions are made. However, I am afraid that for many, such a statement covers over our radical inability, while on this earth, to completely and exhaustively understand the truth revealed by Christ.

Let us adopt the words of the Apostles: To us who are the *least of all* "he has granted of his grace the privilege of proclaiming the *unfathomable* riches of Christ" (Eph. 3:8). Therefore the doctrine of the transcendence of God and his mysteries does not contradict the doctrine of infallibility: indeed by reminding us of our weakness, it keeps that doctrine within proper limits. Furthermore, this transcendence of God makes intellectual immobilism completely impossible for Christians.

Pope Paul VI recognized that doctrinal immobilism is a great obstacle on the road to unity when he quoted these words of Augustine in his talk to the Observers: "Seek in order to find, and find so that you may continue to seek." The Sovereign Pontiff went on to say: "This saying of Augustine applies to all of us, Catholics and non-Catholics alike: the true Christian finds no place for immobilism."

I believe these words point the right way to a solution of doctrinal difficulties. And I would suggest that theological investigation be described in such a fashion that it will not only constantly spur on our separated brothers, but Catholics as well, to a deeper and more accurate expression of the revelation of Christ.

ISAAC GHATTAS

Coptic Bishop of Thebes-Luxor,
Egypt

19

Mixed Marriages

May I give a short explanation of the current practice in the East for the sacrament of *marriage,* to make it clear that the high regard of the Catholic Church for the spiritual heritage of the East can be shown in this chapter only if there is some change in the present practice.

It is a well-known fact that the *sacramental* character of marriage is highly prized not only by Catholics but also by Eastern Orthodox. For countless generations the Catholic Church has acknowledged and honored this Orthodox faith in the sacramental character of marriage by recognizing as valid, *mixed* marriages between Catholics and Orthodox performed before an Orthodox priest. By this traditional practice the Church unquestionably fostered union between Catholics and Orthodox in a very effective way. However, by a decree promulgated May 2, 1949 (*Crebrae allatae*) this practice unfortunately was changed, since the decree declares those mixed marriages invalid which are performed before an Orthodox priest. The decree in no way achieved its intended purpose of preventing mixed marriages, for the number of mixed marriages remains, for all practical purpose, undiminished. Indeed, this decree has harmed religion very considerably, since the number of *invalid* marriages has increased since the promulgation of the decree. In our own area, for instance, it is often difficult or impossible to persuade the partners of a mixed marriage to have the marriage performed before a Catholic priest, since they cannot understand how marriages which were valid and sacramental up to 1949 are now invalid and null by a decree of the Church. This new legislation has, in fact, not only increased the obstacles to union and enlarged the gap of separation, but has also turned quite a few Catholics away from the Church and led some to apostasy.

Therefore I earnestly request the Council, moved by a pastoral spirit and faithful to the spirit of this decree, to restore the marriage practice of Eastern Catholics so that it will be easier for them to be faithful to the Catholic Church. If this is done, the sacramental practice of our Orthodox brothers will be recognized and honored and in this way union between Catholics and Orthodox will be fostered.

PART IV
Dialogue
with the World

POPE PAUL VI
Bishop of Rome

1
The Task

Finally, the Council will build a bridge toward the contemporary world. This is a marvelous thing! The Church seeks to revive her interior life in the Spirit of the Lord and thereby distinguish herself from secular surroundings. At the same time she appears as the life-giving ferment and the instrument of salvation for the world. She reveals and strengthens her missionary vocation. This vocation is to announce the Gospel to the human race—whatever its condition be.

Venerable Brothers, you have experienced this remarkable phenomenon. When you were undertaking the work of the first session, you were inspired by the opening words of Pope John XXIII. You instantly felt the need, as it were, to open the doors of this assembly. You felt the need of suddenly shouting to the world a message of greeting, brotherhood and hope.

What a unique yet admirable gesture this would be! It could be said that the prophetic gift of the Church had suddenly burst into expression. Just as Peter on Pentecost felt an immediate impulse to raise his voice and speak to the people, so you have determined to expand your limited affairs to those of the world. You have determined to conduct a dialogue—not with yourselves, but with the world.

This means, Venerable Brethren, that the present Council is characterized by love, by the most comprehensive and compelling love, by a love which thinks of others even before it thinks of itself—by the universal love of Christ.

This love sustains us now because, as we turn our view to the scene of contemporary human life, we ought to be frightened rather than comforted, saddened rather than gladdened, anxious for defense and condemnation rather than for trust and friendship.

We ought to be realists, not hiding the savagery that from many areas reaches even into this universal synod. Can we be blind and not notice that many seats in this assembly are vacant? Where are our brethren from nations in which the Church is opposed? In what conditions does religion exist in these territories?

At such a reminder our thoughts are aggrieved because of what we know and even more because of what we cannot know about our sacred hierarchy, our men and women religious, our countless children subjected to fear, to persecutions, to privations, to oppression, because of their loyalty to Christ and the Church.

What sadness we feel in the face of such sufferings! What displeasure to see that in certain countries religious liberty, like other fundamental rights of man, is being crushed by principles and methods of political, racial, or anti-religious intolerance! The heart grieves to have to observe that in the world there are still so many acts of injustice against goodness and the free profession of one's religious faith.

But, rather than in bitter words, our lament must be expressed in a frank and human exhortation to all who may be responsible for these evils to put aside with a noble heart their unjustified hostility toward the Catholic religion, whose followers ought to be considered neither as enemies nor as disloyal citizens, but rather as upright and hardworking members of that civil society to which they belong.

Finally, to the Catholics who are suffering for their Faith we send, also on this occasion, our affectionate greetings, and for them we invoke special divine assistance.

Nor does our sorrow end here. The view of the world fills us with crushing sadness because of so many other evils. Atheism is pervading part of the human race and is bringing in its wake the derangement of the intellectual, moral and social orders whose true meaning the world is losing. While the light of the science of nature is increasing, darkness is spreading over the science of God and, in consequence, over man's true science. While progress is perfecting in a wondrous way every kind of instrument that man uses, his heart is declining toward emptiness, sadness and despair.

We have several things to say about these complicated and, for many reasons, sad conditions of modern man. But not today. Now, as we were saying, love is filling our heart and the heart of the Church assembled in Council.

We look upon our times and upon their varied and contrasting manifestations with immense tenderness and with an immense desire to offer to men of today the message of friendship, of salvation and of hope which Christ has brought into the world. "For God did not send his Son into the world in order to judge the world, but that the world might be saved through him" (John 3:17).

Let the world know this: The Church looks at the world with profound understanding, with sincere admiration and with the sincere intention not of dominating it, but of serving it; not of despising it, but of appreciating it; not of condemning it, but of strengthening and saving it.

From the window of the Council, opened wide on the world, the Church looks toward some categories of persons with particular solicitude: It looks toward the poor, the needy, the afflicted, the hungry, the suffering and sorrowing. Humanity belongs to the Church, by the right which the Gospel gives her. She likes to repeat to all who make up the human race: "Come to me, all . . ." (Matt. 11:28).

She looks toward men of culture and learning, scientists, artists. For these also she has great esteem and a great desire to receive the fruit of their experiences, to strengthen their intellectual life, to defend their liberty, to provide a space in which their troubled spirits can expand joyously within the luminous sphere of the divine Word and divine grace.

The Church is concerned for workers, for their persons, for the dignity of their labor and for their legitimate demands. She has concern for their present great and afflicting needs of social improvement and a better spiritual life. Finally, she is concerned about their Christian mission to create a new world order in which men may be free and recognize each other as brothers. The Church, Mother and Teacher, stands beside her workers.

The Church looks to the leaders of the people. Today she substitutes a word of encouragement and trust for serious words of admonition she must often give. Be courageous, rulers of nations! Today you can give your peoples many goods necessary for life: food, education, work, order. You can give them the dignity of free citizens living in harmony. But you must understand what man is—something which only Christian wisdom can tell you with full clarity. Working together in justice and love, you can create peace—this greatest good which all men seek and which the Church so strenuously defends and promotes. From the family of all peoples and races you are able to make one city. May God be with you!

And then the Catholic Church looks further still, beyond the confines of the Christian horizon. For how can she put limits to her love if she would make her own the love of God the Father, who rains down his grace on all men alike (*cf.* Matt. 5:46), and who so loved the world as to give for it his only-begotten Son (*cf.* John 3:16)?

She looks, then, beyond her own sphere and sees these other religions which preserve the sense and notion of the one supreme, transcendent God, Creator and Sustainer, and which worship him with acts of sincere piety and base their moral and social life on their beliefs and religious practices.

It is true that the Catholic Church sees in such religions omissions, insufficiencies and errors which cause her sadness. Yet she cannot exclude them from her thoughts and would have them know that she esteems what they contain of truth and goodness and humanity.

For the Catholic Church is in the forefront of those who, as a necessary duty of true civilization, strive to preserve religion and the worship of God in modern society. She is the most vigorous upholder of God's rights over mankind.

Other vast fields of humanity fall under her gaze: the new generations of youth desirous of living and expressing themselves; the new peoples now coming to self-awareness, independence and civil organization; the innumerable men and women who feel isolated in a troubled society that has no message for their spirit. To all without exception she proclaims the good news of salvation and hope. To all she offers the light of truth and life and salvation. For God "wishes all men to be saved and to come to the knowledge of the truth" (1 Tim. 2:4).

EMILE JOSEPH DE SMEDT

Bishop of Bruges,
Belgium

2
Religious Liberty

Very many conciliar Fathers have insistently demanded that this Sacred Synod clearly explain and proclaim the right of man to religious liberty. Among the reasons given, four principal ones should be listed:

(1) *Truth:* The Church must teach and defend the right to religious liberty because there is a question of the truth, care of which was committed to her by Christ;

(2) *Defense:* The Church cannot remain silent today when almost half of mankind is deprived of religious liberty by atheistic materialism of various kinds;

(3) *Peaceful Social Life:* Today in all nations of the world, men, who adhere to different religions or who lack all religious belief, must live together in one and the same human society; in the light of truth, the Church should point the way toward living together peacefully;

(4) *Ecumenism:* Many non-Catholics harbor an aversion against the Church or at least suspect her of a kind of Machiavellism because we seem to them to demand the free exercise of religion when Catholics are in a minority in any nation

and at the same time refuse and deny the same
religious liberty when Catholics are in the majority.

Religious liberty is such a grave problem in
modern society that it can not be omitted in a
pastoral decree on ecumenism. Therefore, we
submit to your deliberations this fifth chapter of
our schema on ecumenism. The Secretariat for
Promoting Christian Unity, to the best of its ability, has carefully watched over the preparation of
this material.

Since we are treating of a most difficult question
and at the same time one of great importance in
modern life, the authors of the schema cherish the
hope that your attention and pastoral consideration will emend what needs emendment and perfect what is still imperfect in the schema now offered to you.

The term "religious liberty" has a definite
meaning in our text. In the forthcoming discussion, great confusion might arise if any of the
Fathers give to the expression a meaning that
differs from the one intended by the text.

When religious liberty is defended, it is not
asserted that it is proper for man to consider the
religious problem according to his own whim
without any moral obligation and decide for himself according to his own will whether or not to
embrace religion (religious indifferentism).

Nor is it affirmed that the human conscience is
free in the sense that it is as it were outside of the
law, absolved from any obligation toward God
(laicism).

Nor is it said that falsehood is to be considered

on an equal footing with truth, as though there were no objective norm of truth (doctrinal relativism).

Nor is it admitted that man in any way has a quasi-right to maintain a peaceful complacency in the midst of uncertainty (dilettantistic pessimism).

If anyone were to insist upon giving any of the aforesaid meanings to "religious liberty" he would attribute to our text a meaning which neither the words nor our intention possess.

What therefore is meant in the text by "religious liberty"? Positively, religious liberty is the right of the human person to the free exercise of religion according to the dictates of his conscience. Negatively, it is immunity from all external force in his personal relations with God, which the conscience of man vindicates to itself.

Religious liberty implies human autonomy, not from within certainly but from without. From within man is not freed of the obligations toward the religious problem. From without, his liberty is offended when obedience to the dictates of his conscience in religious matters is impeded.

At this point two questions must be asked: (1) can each man claim for himself religious liberty as a sacred right given to him by God? (2) is there, and to what extent is there, a duty on the part of others to recognize the aforesaid religious liberty?

Our decree, since it is pastoral, tries to treat the present matter especially from the practical point of view and, after the manner of John XXIII, will carefully strive to remove the whole question from that world of abstractions which was so dear to the nineteenth century. The question is put therefore regarding real man in his real dealings with other men, in contemporary human and civil societies.

I

The first pastoral problem which must be examined now by this Sacred Synod is this: *how must Catholics because of their faith conduct themselves toward men who do not belong to the Catholic faith?* We propose the following answer for your deliberations:

(1) All Catholics are invited by Christ to strive by prayer, penance, witness and evangelizing in the Holy Spirit to bring our non-Catholic brothers to the blessing of the evangelical light and of the life of the Church. The sacred, absolute right of God as well as the evangelical and natural truths must always and everywhere be honored and observed by them.

(2) They must abstain from all direct coercion. Although God wills all men to be saved and to come to the knowledge of the truth, the disciples of Christ may not infringe upon the religious liberty of the individual person. On the contrary, they must respect and esteem the right and duty of non-Catholics to follow the dictate of their own conscience even when, after sincere and sufficient study, it errs in good faith.

What is the reason of faith why non-Catholics can be forced by no one to admit the Catholic doctrine against their conscience? This reason is to be found in the very nature of the act of faith. For this act, on God's part, is a supernatural gift which the Holy Spirit most freely gives to whom and when he wills: and, on man's part, it is and must be an assent which man freely gives to God.

(3) All Catholics are bound, by the command of the Lord, to love and to help their non-Catholic brothers with a sincere and active charity.

II

At this point, the schema takes a step forward and asserts that each and every man, who follows his conscience in religious matters, has a natural right to true and authentic religious liberty for the whole human family, for all religious groups, for each human person whether his conscience be sincere (*rectam*) and true, or sincere and false concerning faith, provided only that he sincerely follow the dictate of conscience. Therefore, a general principle is laid down: *no human person can be the object of coercion or intolerance.*

What is the reason why observance of religious liberty is demanded of all? The human person endowed with conscious and free activity, since he can fulfill the will of God only as the divine law is perceived through the dictate of conscience, can obtain his ultimate end only by prudently forming the judgment of conscience and by faithfully carrying out its dictate.

From the nature of things, in forming this judgment, whereby man tries freely to conform to the absolute demands of God's rights, neither any other man nor any human institution can take the

place of free judgment of man's conscience.
Therefore, the man who sincerely obeys his own
conscience intends to obey God himself, although
at times confusedly and unknowingly, and is to
be considered worthy of esteem.

When religious liberty is violated, then the very
freedom of the human person is violated in its
principal matter, in a fundamental demand, in
man's ordination to the supreme and ultimate end.
The greatest injury is to prevent a man from wor-
shiping God and obeying God according to the
dictates of his own conscience.

III

The schema takes still another step forward and
enters upon a most difficult question. Religious
liberty would be fruitless and empty if men were
not able to carry out the dictate of their conscience
in external acts whether in private life, in social
life, or in public life, or if human persons were
prevented from forming religious groups whose
members could worship the supreme Deity by
common and social acts and lead a religious life.

Here, however, there arises a most difficult
problem. For, if a human person carries out the
dictates of his conscience by external acts, there
is a danger of violating the rights and duties of
another or of others. Since man is a social being
and since in the human family men are subject
to error and to sin, the conflict of rights and the
conflict of duties cannot always be avoided.
From this it is evident that *the right and duty to
manifest externally the dictate of conscience is*

not unlimited, but can be, at times must be, tempered and regulated for the common good.

This ordering of the common good must be done juridically in human society and belongs to public authority *(potestati publicae).* "One of the fundamental duties of civil authorities, therefore," we read in *Pacem in Terris* (trans. NCWC rev. No. 62) "is to coordinate social relations in such fashion that the exercise of one man's rights does not threaten others in the exercise of their own rights nor hinder them in the fulfillment of their duties. Finally, the rights of all should be effectively safeguarded and, if they have been violated, completely restored."

How is public authority to carry out this duty? In establishing order for the common good, public authority can never act contrary to the order of justice established by God. As St. Thomas says: "Human law is truly law to the extent that it is in accordance with right reason; and therefore it is evident that it is derived from the eternal law. Insofar as it departs from reason, it is a so-called 'wicked law', and therefore is not truly a law but a kind of violence" (I-II, q. 93, a. 3, ad 2um).

Recent Roman Pontiffs again and again have bewailed the fact that not a few governments have gone too far in this matter, ignoring and violating religious liberty. In our own day, there are some regions in which tolerance in religious matters has been so little observed that the Supreme Pontiff, Paul VI, in his allocution to the Fathers of the Second Vatican Council on September 29, 1963, said, speaking of violated right to religious liberty: "Because of sufferings of this kind, with what sadness are we affected, and how deeply we are grieved, when we behold that in some territories religious liberty, together with other principal rights of man, is suppressed by the principles and acts of those who do not tolerate opinions different from theirs on politics, on races of men, or on religion of any kind. We are sorrowed also by many injuries which are done to those who would like to profess their religion honestly and freely."

IV

In order that we might clearly understand the doctrine of the Church on the extent and limits of the civil power's duty relating to religious liberty, we must, in a few words, develop the history of this doctrine. Bear with me, Venerable Fathers, if I seem to make more than just demands on your patience. But the Secretariat for Promoting Christian Unity is convinced that many difficulties and confusions can be avoided in this study of the schema if, before the discussion begins, I show very briefly what the Supreme Pontiffs since the time of Pius IX have taught concerning the duties of public authority in religious matters.

On the question of religious liberty, the principal document is the encyclical *Pacem in Terris* in which Pope John XXIII especially developed these two points of doctrine: (1) by the law of nature, the human person has the right to the free exercise of religion in society according to the dictates of a sincere conscience *(conscientia recta)* whether the conscience be true *(conscientia vera),* or the captive either of error or of inadequate knowledge of truth and of sacred things. (2) To this right corresponds the duty incumbent upon other men and the public authority to recognize and respect that right in such a way that the human person in society is kept immune from all coercion of any kind (*cf. A.A.S.* 55, 1963, p. 299; p. 264 and pp. 273-274).

Moreover, this doctrine must be understood as the contemporary terminus of a process of evolution both in the doctrine on the dignity of the human person and in the Church's pastoral solicitude for man's freedom. This doctrinal evolution took place according to a twofold law:

(1) *Law of continuity:* The Church's doctrine and solicitude are always self-consistent, always remain the same. This perennial doctrine can be expressed in the words of Pope John: "The dignity of the human person demands this, that in his actions man should enjoy his own counsel and freedom" (*ibid,* p. 265). This doctrine has its deepest roots in the Sacred Scriptures which teach that man was made to the image of God. From this doctrine stems the continual pastoral solicitude of the Church for man's true freedom.

(2) *Law of progress:* The ecclesiastical magisterium adapts, explains, and defends genuine doctrine according to the demands of errors which are spread and according to the needs which arise from the development of man and of society. By this progress, the mind of the Church is led to search more deeply into doctrine and to understand it more clearly.

In this way, there has arisen in two areas a distinction which no one has explained more clearly than Pope John XXIII in his encyclical *Pacem in*

Terris: (1) A clearer distinction between false *philosophical teachings* and the *endeavors and institutions* which these ideologies give rise to or nourish. While on the one hand the ideologies are always to be condemned, on the other hand the economic, social and civil institutions which have arisen therefrom can contain something that is good and worthy of approval. (2) A clearer distinction between *errors* and the *person* who errs in good faith. While on the one hand errors must always be rejected, on the other hand the man in error "does not cease to be endowed with human nature, nor does he ever lose his dignity as a person, due consideration of which must always be maintained (*ibid.* pp. 299-300).

These two laws of continuity and progress must be kept before our eyes always when the documents of the Apostolic See are read and interpreted.

V

In this way the door is opened to a correct understanding of many pontifical documents which in the nineteenth century treated of religious liberty in such words that this liberty appeared as something that had to be condemned. The clearest example is found in the encyclical *Quanta Cura* of Pius IX, in which we read: "From this completely false concept of social rule (naturalism), they do not hesitate to foster that erroneous opinion which is especially injurious to the Catholic Church and the salvation of souls, called by our predecessor Gregory XVI *"deliramentum"*, namely that freedom of conscience and of cults is the proper right of each man, and this should be proclaimed and asserted in every rightly constituted society" (*A.S.S.* 3, 1867, p. 162).

As is evident, this freedom of conscience is condemned because of the ideology of the rationalists who founded their conclusions upon the principle that the individual conscience is under no law, and therefore, is subject to no divinely given norms. (*Cf. Syllabus,* prop. 3, *A.S.S.* 3, p. 168). Freedom of worship is condemned also when it is based upon religious indifferentism (*ibid.* prop. 15, p. 170). Finally there is condemned that separation of the Church from the State which is based upon the rationalistic principle of the juridical omnicompetence of the State, according to which the Church is to be incorporated into the monistic organism of the State and is to be subjected to its supreme authority (*ibid.,* prop. 39, p. 172).

To understand those condemnations correctly, we must see in them the constant doctrine and solicitude of the Church concerning the true dignity of the human person and his true liberty (law of continuity). For the ultimate basis of human dignity lies in the fact that man is a creature of God. He is not God himself, but an image of God. From this absolute dependence of man upon God there flows every right and duty of man to claim for himself and for others true religious liberty. For man is subjectively bound to worship God according to the sincere dictates of his own conscience *(juxta rectam suae conscientiae normam)* because objectively he is absolutely dependent upon God.

In order, therefore, that his absolute dependence upon God might not be infringed in any way,
man must not be impeded in any way by others
or even by public authority from freely practicing
his religion. Therefore, in opposing the philosophical and political tenets of laicism, the Church
was fighting for the dignity and true liberty of the
human person. In accordance with the law of continuity, then, the Church, in spite of changing
conditions, has remained consistent both in the
past and in the present.

Leo XIII had already started this doctrinal development when he distinguished clearly between
the Church, the people of God, and the civil
society, a terrestrial and temporal people (*cf.
Immortale Dei, A.S.S.* 18, 1885, pp. 166-167).
By this means, he opened the way to a new affirmation of the due and lawful autonomy which belongs to the civil order and to its juridical dis-
positions. Because of this, it was possible to take
a step forward (law of progress) toward a new
judgment on "modern freedoms".

These freedoms can be tolerated (*cf. ibid.*, p.
174: *Libertas Praestantissimum A.S.S.* 20, 1887,
pp. 609-610). And yet they were to be *tolerated*
only. The reason was evident. For at that time in
Europe the regimes which proclaimed the modern
freedoms, religious liberty among them, consciously drew their inspiration from the laicist
ideology. There was danger, therefore—Leo
XIII sensed this—that the civil and political institutions of this kind of republic, since they were
of laicist orientation, would lead to such abuses
that they would necessarily do violence to the dig-

nity and true liberty of the human person. In accordance with the law of continuity, what was dear to Leo XIII is always dear to the Church— the safeguarding of the human person.

With the rise of State-totalitarianism in its various forms, Pope Pius XI brought pastoral and doctrinal development to a new height. There is no longer any danger, as there was in the nineteenth century, that the false concept of liberty might do violence to human dignity. There is a new danger, that every kind of human and civil liberty, and above all religious liberty, will be destroyed. For this reason, the Church is beginning in a new way to manifest her concern, which through the centuries has never wavered, for human liberty and dignity. With the increase of her pastoral concern, the Church's doctrine continues to develop.

Faithfully observing the law of continuity, Pius XI maintained the unstinting opposition of the Church to anti-religious laicism: "Those things which Pius X condemned we also condemn: as often as there is in 'laicism' any meaning or purpose that is harmful or contrary to God or religion, we condemn laicism, and openly declare that it must be condemned, as alien to God and religion" (*Maximam Gravissimamque, A.A.S.* 16, 1924, p. 10).

But observing the rule of progress no less, Pius XI introduced a new distinction which was of great importance for a deeper understanding of Catholic doctrine. He made a distinction between the "freedom of conscience" and the "freedom of consciences". The former he rejected as "equivocal" as often used by the laicist to signify "an absolute independence of conscience, which is an absurdity in man who was created and redeemed by God"; the latter however, "freedom of consciences", he accepted, stating that he would joyfully fight the good fight for "freedom of consciences" (*Non abbiamo bisogno, A.A.S.* 23, 1931, pp. 301-302).

Moreover, Pius XI not only fought for the religious liberty of the faithful, but he was at the same time compelled to show pastoral concern on a wider basis. For not only the Christian, but human reality was at stake, if we can rightly distinguish between two things that are in reality one.

By way of new advances, Pius XI developed a truly liberal and Christian doctrine when he taught: "man as a person possesses God-given rights which must remain immune from all denial, privation, or interference on the part of society" (*Mit brennender Sorge, A.A.S.* 29, 1937, p. 159). And he continues in no ambiguous words: "The believer possesses the inalienable right to profess his faith and to practice it in a proper way. Laws which interfere with or render difficult this profession and practice are in contradiction to the natural law" (*ibid.* p. 160). No one who understands the condition of the times and the purpose of this encyclical can fail to understand the universal intent of this statement.

Deeply sharing the pastoral solicitude of his predecessor, Pius XII developed further and expanded his doctrine (law of progress). One thing he kept before his mind, the human person, created by God, redeemed by Christ Jesus, yet placed in stringent circumstances and surrounded on all sides by dangers.

In this context of doctrine and pastoral solicitude (law of continuity) we must read the text which in this matter is supreme. Enumerating "the fundamental rights of the person" which must be recognized and respected in every well-ordered society, he repeats the doctrine of Pius XI and vests it with new authority, affirming "the right to the private and public worship of God, including *'actio caritativa'* " (*Nuntius radiophonicus,* 24 Dec. 1942, *A.A.S.* 35, 1943, p.19).

The Roman Pontiff did not propose this doctrine as a tenuous opinion or as a theory belonging to the schools. On the contrary, he carries the doctrine to its juridical conclusions so that it becomes a principle according to which just limits are placed on public authority: "The chief duty of any public authority is to safeguard the inviolable rights that are proper to men and so to provide that each one might more easily fulfill his duties" (*Nuntius radiophonicus,* 1 June 1941, *A.A.S.* 33, 1941, p. 200).

Here we must recall especially the doctrine of Pius XII on the limitation of the State, because it deals with the suppression of errors within society: "Could it be that in certain circumstances he (God) would not give men any mandate, would not impose any duty, and would not even communicate the right to impede or to repress what is erroneous and false? A look at things as they are gives an affirmative answer." Then having cited the example of divine providence, he proceeds: "Hence the affirmation: religious and

moral error must always be impeded, when it is
possible, because toleration of them is in itself
immoral, is not valid absolutely and unconditionally. Moreover, God has not given even to human
authority such an absolute and universal command in matters of faith and morality. Such a
command is unknown to the common convictions
of mankind, to Christian conscience, to the
sources of revelation, and to the practice of the
Church" (*Ci riesce, A.A.S.* 45, 1953, pp. 798-
799).

This declaration (law of progress) is of the
greatest importance for our question, especially
if we keep in mind what was in the past held concerning the role of the State.

At the end of this historical development comes
the encyclical *Pacem in Terris*. This document
comes forth as a ripe fruit of a slow process of
growth which has taken place within the Church,
under the light of the Holy Spirit, throughout the
whole of the last century.

Our schema had already been prepared and had
been studied by the Central Commission and by
the Commission for Coordination when Pope
John, on April 11 of this year, published his last
encyclical *Pacem in Terris*. We believe that our
text is in complete conformity with his pellucid
doctrine, which was received within the Church
and outside the Church with unprecedented
praise.

We now submit for your consideration this text.
In the historical conspectus of this doctrine, we
have shown that in the pontifical documents, along
with continuity, we must look for a progressive

spelling-out of doctrine. It is evident that certain quotations from the popes, because of a difference in words, can be put in opposition to our schema. But I beseech you, Venerable Fathers, not to force the text to speak outside of its historical and doctrinal context, not in other words to make the fish swim out of water.

Let our document be studied as it stands. It is not a dogmatic treatise, but a pastoral decree directed to men of our time. The whole world is waiting for this decree. The voice of the Church on religious liberty is being waited for in universities, in national and international organizations, in Christian and non-Christian communities, in the newspapers, and in public opinion—and it is being waited for with urgent expectancy.

We hope that it will be possible to complete the discussion and the approbation of this very brief, but very important, decree before the end of this second session. How fruitful our work would appear to the world if the conciliar Fathers, with the voice of Peter's successor, could announce this liberating doctrine on religious liberty!

Venerable Fathers, we will add our labors to yours. Our Secretariat will study your emendations most attentively and also with the utmost speed. We will work day and night. But our hope is in the Lord. May Jesus Christ assist all of us with his grace. If at the end of this session he asks of us: "Young men, do you have any fish?" seeing the faith and good will of this Council, he might say to their successors what once he said to the Apostles: "Cast the net to the right of the boat: and you will find" (John 21:6).

CARDINAL AUGUSTINE BEA

President of the Secretariat
for Christian Unity

3

Catholics and Jews

The schema "On Jews" now up for examination was begun about two years ago and in substance it was finished in May of last year. This year, with the approval of the Council Coordinating Committee, it was placed in the schema "On Ecumenism."

The Secretariat to which the care of promoting Christian Unity is given undertook the question treating the Jews not on its own initiative, but by reason of the express command of the Supreme Pontiff, Pope John XXIII of happy memory. This was given verbally to the president of the Secretariat.

After this schema was prepared, it was to be discussed in the conferences of the Central Commission in June 1962. The discussion was omitted not because of the ideas or doctrine expressed in the schema, but only because of certain unhappy political conditions at that time.

The decree is very brief, but the material treated in it is not easy. Let us enter immediately into the heart of it and tell what we are talking about. Or rather, since it is so easy to understand it wrongly, before all else let us say what we are not talking about. There is no national nor political question

here. Especially is there no question of acknowledging the State of Israel on the part of the Holy
See. None of these questions is treated in the
schema. Nor is there any treatment of such condition or consideration in any way. There is only
treatment of a purely religious question.

The decree intends to recall in a solemn way
those things which the Church of Christ by hidden design of divine providence, receives through
the hands of the chosen people of Israel. It receives especially, in the words of St. Paul in his
epistle to the Romans, "the oracles of God"
(Rom. 3:2); that is, the word of God in the Old
Testament. Besides, in the words of the same St.
Paul, they "are Israelites, who have the adoption
as sons, and the glory and the covenants, and the
legislation and the worship and the promises";
who have the fathers and from whom "is Christ
according to the flesh, who is over all things, God,
blessed forever" (Rom. 9:4-5).

In other words, not only was the whole preparation of the work of the redeemer and his Church
done in the Old Testament, but also the execution
of his work, the foundation of the Church and its
propagation in the world, either in the chosen
people of Israel or through members of this people
whom God chose as instruments. The Church is
in some sense the continuation of the chosen people of Israel, as is so well stated in the schema on
the Church, so that according to St. Paul, Christians can be called "Israelites" not indeed "according to the flesh" but because in them are fulfilled
the promises made to Abraham, the father of the
people of Israel (*cf.* Rom. 9:6-8). For in us

Christians, members of the Church, the perfection of that kingdom of God for which God selected and designated the people of Israel, is brought to fruition.

Really, it is a valid question to ask whether our preachers at times in their sermons, especially on the passion of our Lord, use these facts and associations of the Church to the chosen people of Israel and whether they give our necessary thanks to this people.

There are those who object: Did not the princes of this people with the people in agreement, condemn and crucify the innocent Christ, the Lord? Did they not "clamor": "Let his blood be upon us and upon our children" (Matt. 27:25)? Did not Christ himself speak most severely about Jews and their punishment?

I reply simply and briefly: It is true that Christ spoke severely, but only with the intention that the people might be converted and might "recognize the time of its visitation" (*cf.* Luke 19:42-49). But even as he is dying on the cross he prays: "Father forgive them, for they know not what they do" (Luke 23:34).

Wherefore, since the Lord emphasized, before the burial of Lazarus, speaking to the Father: "I know that thou always hearest me" (John 11:42), it is wrong to say that his prayer to the Father was not heard and that God has not only not forgiven the fault of his chosen people but that he has rejected them.

God himself through St. Paul assures us that he "in no way" has rejected his chosen and beloved people. For the Apostle writes to the Romans:

"I say then: has God cast off his people? By no means . . . God has not cast off his people whom he foreknew" (Rom. 11:1-2). And a little below this he gives the reason: "For the gifts and the call of God are without repentance" (*ibid,* v. 29), that is, God does not revoke a choice once made nor does he reject the people of Israel. Going still further, St. Paul affirms that at some time "all Israel" will be saved, both those who are of "Israel according to the flesh" as well as those who are of Israel according to the promise only. For the Apostle states: "For I would not, brethren, have you ignorant of this mystery, lest you should be wise in your own conceits, that a partial blindness only has befallen Israel, until the full number of the gentiles should enter and thus all Israel should be saved . . . for as you [the Romans, insofar as they belonged to the non-Jewish people] also at one time did not believe God, but now have obtained mercy by reason of their unbelief, so too they have now not believed by reason of the mercy shown you, that they too may obtain mercy" (Rom. 11:25-30).

Hence St. Paul, who indeed suffered so much from some Jews, having imitated the burning charity of God, said: "For I could wish to be anathema myself from Christ for the sake of my brethren, who are my kinsmen according to the flesh" (Rom. 9:3).

Therefore, the aim of this very brief decree is to call to the attention of Christ's faithful these truths concerning the Jews proposed by the Apostle and contained in the deposit of faith and to do this so clearly that in dealing with the children of that people the faithful will act in no other way than did Christ the Lord and his Apostles, Peter and Paul. St. Peter in preaching to the Jewish people on the crucifixion of the Lord said: "I know that you did this through ignorance as did your leaders . . ." (Acts 3:17). Thus he excuses even the leaders themselves. Likewise St. Paul (Acts 13:27).

The point, therefore, is not in any way to call into doubt—as is sometimes falsely asserted—the events which are narrated in the Gospels about Christ's consciousness of his dignity and divine nature, or about the manner in which the innocent Lord was unjustly condemned. Rather that, with these things kept fully in mind, it is still possible and necessary to imitate the gentle charity of Christ the Lord and his Apostles with which they excused their persecutors.

But *why is it so necessary precisely today* to recall these things? The reason is this. Some decades ago anti-Semitism, as it is called, was prevalent in various regions and in a particularly violent and criminal form, especially in Germany under the rule of National Socialism, which through hatred for the Jews committed frightful crimes, extirpating several millions of Jewish people—we need not at the moment seek the exact number. Moreover, accompanying and assisting this whole activity was a most powerful and effective "propaganda" as it is called, against the Jews. Now it would have been almost impossible if some of the claims of that propaganda did not have an unfortunate effect even on the faithful Catholics, the more so since the arguments advanced by that propaganda often enough bore the appearance of truth, especially when they were drawn from the New Testament and from the history of the Church. Thus, since the Church in this Council is striving to renew itself by "seeking again the outlines of its most fervent youth" as John XXIII of venerable memory said (*cf.* Discourse of November 14, 1960, *A.A.S.* 52, 1960, 960), it seems imperative to take up this question.

Not that anti-Semitism, especially that of National Socialism, drew its inspiration from Christian doctrine, something which is in no way true. Rather, it is a question of rooting out from the minds of Catholics any ideas which perhaps remain fixed there through the influence of that propaganda. If Christ the Lord and the Apostles who personally experienced the sorrows of the crucifixion embraced their very persecutors with an ardent charity, how much more must we be motivated by the same charity?

For the Jews of our times can hardly be accused of the crimes committed against Christ, so far removed are they from those deeds. Actually, even in the time of Christ, the majority of the chosen people did not cooperate with the leaders of the people in condemning Christ. Does not the Gospel say that an actual member of the Sanhedrin, namely, Joseph of Arimethea, did not agree "to their plan and their actions" (Luke 23:51)? Again those among them who cried out to Pilate "Crucify him" formed a very small part of the chosen people. Were not the leaders of the Jews unwilling to kill the Lord "on the feast day lest there be tumult among the people" (Matt. 26:5)?

If therefore not even all the Jews in Palestine
or in Jerusalem could be accused, how much less
the Jews dispersed throughout the Roman Empire? And how much less again those who today
after nineteen centuries live scattered in the whole
world.

But let us set aside these considerations. Let
the example of ardent charity given by the Lord
and the Apostles be sufficient for us. To this example the Church must conform as perfectly as
possible in teaching the passion and death of the
Lord. In saying this we do not mean to state or to
hint that anti-Semitism usually or principally arises
from a religious source, namely from what the
Gospels recount concerning the passion and death
of the Lord. We know very well that anti-Semitism
also has causes of a political-national, psychologi-
cal, social and economic nature. But we affirm
that the Church most certainly must imitate
Christ's example of gentle charity toward the people through whom it received so many great benefits from God.

If and when, therefore, some or many Jews do
this or that one of the things of which they are
accused, Christians will be mindful of the example of St. Paul. He, while violently attacked by
many of the Jews, indeed publicly denounced his
persecutors who were interfering with either his
freedom to announce the Word of the Lord or the
freedom of men to believe the Gospel (cf. 1 Thess.
2:15f). At the same time, however, he testified
that he loved them so ardently that he would wish
"to be anathema from Christ" for them. In such
fashion, therefore, the children of the Church also

should make vigorous use of the peaceful weapons of truth, charity and patience, which weapons are surely most effective.

Lastly: since we are here treating a merely religious question, there is obviously no danger that the Council will get entangled in those difficult questions regarding the relations between the Arab nations and the State of Israel, or regarding so-called Zionism.

In December of last year, I set out in writing for the Supreme Pontiff, Pope John XXIII of happy memory, a discussion of this question "Regarding the Jews". After a few days the Holy Father indicated to me his full approval.

The Supreme Pontiff himself did indeed write in this way scarcely five months before his holy death. Certainly, I am not saying that the question which we are treating was settled by these words of his; for he wanted the Council to be free, just as his successor also unquestionably wishes it. I think, however, that these words of his are dear to all the Most Eminent and Most Excellent Fathers, and that at the same time, they throw light on how to follow the Lord Christ.

However, for our purpose, of much more importance, in fact simply decisive, is the example of burning charity of the Lord himself on the cross praying "Father, forgive them, for they know not what they are doing". This is the example to be imitated by the Church, the bride of Christ. This is the road to be followed by her. This is what the schema proposed by us intends to foster and promote.

ROBERT E. TRACY

Bishop of Baton Rouge,
United States

4
No Racial Discrimination

In the name of the bishops of the United States of North America I want to suggest that in speaking of the people of God, we put clearer emphasis on the equality of everyone in the Church with no distinction on account of race.

Here are the reasons for the suggestion.

1. If the Council does this, it will more concretely and explicitly show that equality which all the members of the people of God rightfully possess. Furthermore all discrimination based on race alone is completely irreconcilable with the truth which we believe, namely that God has created all men with equal rights and dignity.

2. In this way we will be more fully in harmony with that text of St. Paul where he wants to insist that all opposition between "Jew" and "Greek" has now disappeared. For it is more accurate to understand the terms "Jew" and "Greek" here as referring to distinction on the basis of religion, culture—and race, rather than nation.

3. Because of the present situation in the United States and also, *mutatis mutandis,* in other areas, the Council Fathers are often faced with this problem of race prejudice. The bishops of the United States have repeatedly issued public statements explaining this doctrine in an effort to teach the people social justice and love. Now, if the Council issues a solemn and concrete affirmation of the equality of all races, it will greatly help the bishops to teach their people more effectively.

4. Even though these problems are confined to certain geographical areas, their echo and effect make this an international problem worthy of action by the Council.

5. Such a statement by the Council would bring great consolation to all those who are deprived of equal liberty and humiliated and oppressed under the yoke of prejudice for no other reason than their race.

6. A statement of this kind from the Council will also provide the doctrinal basis for future decrees which will perhaps apply the principle of equality of all peoples more fully and in greater detail to modern needs. Therefore, for these reasons, which concern a problem which is pastoral in a very special way and is urgent in our times, we ask that a solemn dogmatic declaration of the equality of all men, of whatever people or race, be included in the chapter on the people of God.

MARK McGRATH

Auxiliary Bishop of Panama,
Panama

5
The
Responsible Layman
in the World

Fifty years ago the editors of the Code of Canon Law barely mentioned the layman in it. But now in the Council we are speaking about him at great length to find the right place and manner of speaking about the layman within the principal Constitution, on the Church. This surely makes it clear that progress on the question of the layman is an essential part of the whole renewal (*aggiornamento*) of the Church which everyone looks forward to so eagerly. I think that this is a source of joy for us all.

Yet there are still many, not only laymen, but theological experts and even bishops, who, studying this chapter, find that it does not adequately express the role of the layman and therefore has too clerical a ring. Why do they say this?

The description of the supernatural life which all Christians share, in the section dealing with the people of God, is very beautifully done. But all of this needs to be incarnated in the concrete circumstances of everyone's role in the Church. For the hierarchy and clergy this is done in the chapter on the structure of the Church; for those who follow the counsels there is a treatment in the chapter on the vocation to holiness. Now in this chapter application should be made for the layman, at least in those matters which touch upon his life and apostolate, leaving the question of holiness to another chapter. But in our chapter as it stands this application falls short in many ways.

1. *Definition of the layman.* The definition of the layman which is proposed seems inadequate. For when the layman is negatively defined as that baptized person who does not belong either to the hierarchy or to a religious state approved by the Church, such a definition, framed in terms of two states on entirely different levels, is quite inadequate. For the hierarchy is something of the sacramental order, while the religious state involves a a way of striving toward perfection. Several confusions arise out of this defective definition, for example, that religious are never laymen, even when they do not have sacred orders, which is false. Therefore it would be better simply to change the text of the definition to read "This Sacred Synod teaches that laymen are those of the faithful who, having been incorporated into the people of God by baptism, serve God in the normal state of believing Christians and according to their situation carry on in the world the mission of the whole Christian people, but are not part of the hierarchy."

2. *The lay apostolate.* The texts of the Constitution consider the layman too exclusively in connection with the apostolate. Is not what a man is more primary and basic than what he does? But the layman's life is scarcely considered in itself as an instrument of the apostolate—and apostolate is understood here in the strict sense, that is, what is done under the "mandate" of the hierarchy, and touches on religion either directly or indirectly. It is true that there are a few remarks about the temporal task of the layman, and indeed this notion is given explicit treatment, but before the idea is adequately explained it is again drawn into the context of the hierarchy.

Such a hobbled description builds up an unreal picture of the Church where the whole life of the Christian seems to be summed up in submission to the hierarchy, in some kind of clerical pyramid where the layman stands on the bottom step like a tiny acolyte subject to everyone else. Or, to put it another way, the whole life of the Church in the world would be as we are today in this Council hall: manifest principally in the episcopacy, then in the clergy, and finally completed by a small band of laymen who serve us in our work.

It is evident that images such as these are unreal because they fail to give the full reality of the Church, and this just because the whole Christian life of the layman is not summed up in his relation to the apostolate of the hierarchy, even though this collaboration of the laity in works which are directly or indirectly religious is of the highest importance, especially in our areas where priests are so few. Actually, many laymen, indeed most of them by far, have no time or at the best very little to give to the apostolate of the hierarchy either on account of their poverty or because of their vocation to secular tasks. Instead most of them are busy the whole time with so-called worldly affairs. There are certainly moral values in all these things and the layman is obliged in conscience to perform his task in accordance with the moral law. But, for this he rarely needs the intervention of the hierarchy. His properly-formed conscience is all he needs to act prudently, and the task of the clergy is to form that conscience according to the mind of Christ rather than to make every judgment for the layman. In fact it is the layman who has authority even over us bishops in all merely secular activities and offices: the doctor, for instance, the police, the mayor, all of whom we must obey in their area of authority just as they obey us in religious matters. In other words, there is no reason for a Christian civilization to be ecclesiastical, much less clerical.

This may seem to be too obvious and simple a statement; but it holds a great truth. We bishops and priests can easily look at everything in terms of the religious apostolate in which we are placed as pastors of the Lord's flock. As a consequence of this we easily lose a sense for the natural values of things. Etienne Gilson used to say: "To offer our knowledge to God is a good thing" but "if something is genuinely and truly to be offered to God, the first prerequisite is that it really be knowledge," otherwise nothing is offered to God. All of us, simply as men, even apart from baptism, have the task of organizing this world in a genuinely

human way. This is very important if we are to
avoid the temptation to make light of the internal
laws of the world of culture, society and the
sciences. We may and must recognize that true
secular values exist in a real sense for Christians.
The layman must not—under the pretext of some
kind of deep religiosity—despise these values, but
must devote all his energies to making the order
of creation constantly better, in accordance with
the Christological principle: "what is not taken
up [by Christ] is not healed". In the field of natural science and natural virtues Catholics may and
should act together with all men of good will, as
the encyclicals of the Sovereign Pontiffs so clearly
insist in paragraph after paragraph. It is too bad
that Catholics are less outstanding in these areas
than their numbers give us a right to expect.
Is not the reason for this that we have spoken to
them too exclusively about the religious apostolate
and have said little about what is simply human?
This becomes even more serious in our time when
technical progress and the new scientific mentality
are dominant, and at the same time growing
masses of humanity in many regions live in misery.
The gospel is not preached in a vacuum. The
great problems which preoccupy men now in our
regions of Latin America are just those problems
of the progress they dream of and the real misery
in which they find themselves. They are striving
manfully to build an earthly city more in accordance with human dignity and freedom. But far
too often in this situation the Church seems pre-
occupied only with supernatural realities; this exclusive concern for the supernatural looks very

much like that "philosophy of evasion" of which Cardinal Gracias spoke. Furthermore, in these regions the Church often seems to be closely tied to the "old order"—whether intellectual or social. If we, then, cannot show the human and Christian meaning of this progress of mankind, if we do not make it immediately clear that man's labor contributes to justice and love among men, so that it is somehow a distant preparation or foreshadowing of the Kingdom of God in the mutual service of the things men enjoy in this life, so that they may have a truly human existence; if we are incapable of proposing a theology of these so-called earthly realities; if our faith, enlivened by love, does not show itself in deed and truth through social effects, there is a great danger that in the "new areas of the world" the next generation will become materialists. But if we can reach this new world with the Christian ideal of love and justice, in which all true progress is better understood and more eagerly desired, we will be able to achieve the final goal set for the Council by the Sovereign Pontiff Paul VI, which is for the Church to "build a bridge to the contemporary world" (Address of September 29, 1963).

That, in brief, is the problem. I completely agree with the remarks of Bishop Hervas. A lay apostolate which does not spring from grace and love is worthless and will soon die. It is just those great wonders of the supernatural life that we must share more fully with the layman, a task which is accomplished so well in the *Cursillos de Cristiandad* founded by the same Bishop Hervas, so that the new people of God may consecrate the world to its Lord in hymns of praise and glory. But this does not happen in a vacuum, or only in a church or sacristy. Instead, Christian men, who are fortified with faith and the sacraments of the Church, work more intensely in the world and earn there by the sweat of their brows their own salvation and that of their neighbor. The holiness of the people of God must be planted in their real world; and their royal priesthood must be employed to subdue the world for the glory of God and the service of men.

6

The Church
and Non-Christian
Religions

1. *Preliminary remarks.* Although the schema on the Church is good, it seems to need improvement by making the following points stand out more clearly: *the full extent of God's redemptive plan,* not only for individuals but also for whole societies and non-Christian religions; the *openness of the Church* and missionary work to all positive elements outside Christianity; *the constructive building spirit* which should inspire missionaries and missionary work.

The alternative text we present here will deal with the *general theology* of the Church and the non-Christian world, since this is not the place for detailed treatment.

We shall make use of many *biblical texts,* especially from those sections where the divine plan for non-Christians is clarified, such as: Peter's words to Cornelius (Acts 10); Paul's speech to the Athenians (Acts 17); his teaching about the pagans (Rom.); the mystery of universal redemption in Christ (Eph., Col.).

The development of our text has four parts: a short account of the universal function of the incarnate Word and the Church; a correlative description of the universal religious aspiration toward the "unknown God"; a demonstration of how it follows that all non-Christian values must be accepted and elevated in the Church; a clarification, as a result of all this, of the style and goal of the mission among non-Christians.

2. *The suggested text.*

(1) Since the Church is the Spouse and Body of Christ, the universal Redeemer who "the first to rise from the dead, proclaims light both to Israel and to the Gentiles" (Acts 26:23), she too, by her very nature, should "proclaim to the Gentiles the good news of the unfathomable riches of Christ and bring to light how this hidden purpose is to be put into effect, this purpose which was hidden for long ages in God" (Eph.3:8-9), "giving the good news of peace through Jesus Christ" (Acts 10:36).

Jesus himself pointed to this essential mission when he commanded his Apostles "go forth to every part of the world and proclaim the good news to the whole creation" (Mark 16:15) and "make all nations my disciples, baptize men everywhere" (Matt. 28:19).

Therefore the Church, making her own the words of Paul, "Woe to me if I do not preach the Gospel" (1 Cor. 9:16), may take no respite from the task of preaching the Gospel to the whole

*world, by prayer, by the witness of holiness, by
the practice of love, and especially by apostolic
work among non-Christians, until all men, especially the poor, are brought together into the one
Body of Christ.*

*(2) In this way she meets the needs and desires
of the whole human family: "For all alike have
sinned, and are deprived of the divine splendor"
(Rom. 3:23). And God "created every race of
men of one stock, to inhabit the whole earth's
surface . . . to seek him, and, it might be, touch
and find him" (Acts 17:27). Indeed "he is not
far from each one of us" (Acts 17:27); "his invisible attributes have been visible, ever since the
world began, to the eye of reason, in the things
he has made" (Rom. 1:20). "Although they have
no law, they are their own law . . . their conscience is called as a witness" (Rom. 2:14-15). In
every religion, in every people, there were religious men who worshiped the unknown God in
temples or in their hearts . . .*

*(3) Those who try to live in spirit and truth
according to the dictates of their conscience are
faithful to the divine will. Everything good, everything holy in non-Christian men and groups of
men prepares the way for the Gospel; it all points
to Christ "on whom faith depends from start to
finish" (Heb. 12:12), and it can and should be
taken and raised to a higher level by him through
the Church.*

*(4) Therefore, for them to come to the full
light which is the light of Christian revelation, it
is urgently necessary for them to "know him who
alone is truly God and Jesus Christ whom he has*

sent (John 17:3), and in this way they will be led to the Body of Christ, which is the Church, by the help of the same God.

Everyone, then, who is sent by the Church to non-Christians should make it his concern to be "a minister of Jesus Christ to the Gentiles with God's gospel for his priestly charge, so that the offering of the Gentiles to him may be acceptable, sanctified by the Holy Spirit" (Rom. 15:16). In this way the authentic religious heritage of every religion, state, or person not only will not be destroyed in being offered to God, but will be raised to a more lofty and final dignity. It will contribute to the splendor of the Church, which should be progressively enriched with a greater variety of peoples. It will contribute to the fullness of the Body of Christ, in which "all are to be brought into a unity" (Eph. 1:10), until he "delivers up the Kingdom to God the Father" (1 Cor. 15:24).

JOHN-BAPTIST ZOA

Archbishop of Yaounde,
Cameroun

7

United Witness
of All Christians

The twentieth century is struggling to find its unity.

Since the Catholic Church possesses promises of a unity of the human family in the Body of Christ, she is very concerned about this expectant hope, to which, in the power of Christ, she wants to provide the answer.

There are two elements related in a special way to this hope: (1) the ecumenical effort, which is a movement to gather and reunite once again the separated members of the Christian family; (2) the missionary movement, out of which new Churches are born and grow, linked by the bond of love to the Churches of Europe and America.

The Church must at the same time foster both the missionary and the ecumenical movements. Since Christ came into the world to proclaim the good news of salvation to men and thus to call them into the unity of his Body, the missionary movement calls to unity and unity gives rise to mission. This makes it clear that those regions in which there is missionary preaching must foster the ecumenical effort and those regions where ecumenism flourishes cannot be without preaching which proclaims the good news. We have repeatedly seen that the division of Christians is a great scandal for unbelievers and a most serious obstacle to the evangelization of the whole world.

For we know that the beginning of the ecumenical movement among our Christian brothers came from the missions who wanted to witness together to Christ in the world and work together, better to show the love of Christ. This message of theirs still remains true today. The stimulus of the whole ecumenical movement now organized in the World Council of Churches comes mainly from a missionary spirit; indeed, it springs from this spirit, all its efforts are aimed at fulfilling it. We too, vying with the love of our brothers, should earnestly beg Christ to bring us all closer together. This is a question which concerns the evangelization of our regions.

We rejoice that in recent years we have met together and carried on discussions with Protestants in a spirit of brotherhood. We rejoice in these contacts at this historic moment when the whole of Africa is striving to manifest its unity, for harmony among Christians is a very challenging sign for other men. We rejoice at the meetings of the African Protestant Churches in Hadan and Kampala, because they show more and more clearly how much we need the ecumenical dialogue. We beg Christ to create a true unity between us.

In these circumstances the schema on ecumenism seems to us to be an extremely important contribution to the work of restoring Christian unity.

I conclude with three suggestions:

1. Since modern states must solve the great problems of contemporary life, it is desirable that, as far as possible, Christians unite to witness together in those matters where they all agree. A shared witness is more meaningful and carries more weight.

2. In cultural, ethnological, and social matters, which are so desperately important for the younger Churches, it is useful, as the meeting at Abidjan clearly showed, to share our experience and thoughts in a spirit of brotherhood. Both Catholic and Protestant theologians and missionaries hope that cooperation between Protestant missionaries and Catholic groups in studies of non-Christian religions and of African and Asian mentalities and social patterns may be worked out in a practical way. This hope must not be frustrated.

3. To avoid the kind of competition in specifically ecclesiastical matters which is not in the spirit of the Gospel, it would be desirable to create in Africa some means of information and consultation among the different Christian communions. In this way the path will gradually be opened for a study in the spirit of brotherhood of those doctrinal issues which separate us. This will make it easier for us to avoid syncretism, which is such a common danger for all Christian communions in Africa. Ecumenism is no obstacle to the missionary work of the Church. On the contrary, it is

really the *indispensable condition* of all true witness in the contemporary world to the mystery of Christ. Before they will believe in Christ, people must see that Christians, even those who are still separated, have love for one another.

EUGENE D'SOUZA

Archbishop of Bhopal,
India

8

The
Missionary Task
of the Church

I speak in the name of the bishops of the ecclesiastical provinces of Delhi, Agra, Calcutta, Ranchi, Nagpur and Bhopal in North India.

We hear it said that the Church may not rest from prayer and preaching until all are gathered together into her one body. It is certainly timely to turn our attention to the supreme responsibility of preaching the Gospel to the whole world, a responsibility which the Church has by her very nature. However it seems to us that we must show more clearly and state more unequivocally that this responsibility is shared by the *whole Church* and rests in a special way with the *whole episcopal college*. It may not be simply delegated to one part of it.

We are surprised and also saddened that the schema on the missions is not yet ready. Some say that a special schema on the missions is superfluous. Is not the task of spreading the Gospel, they say, an integral part of the very life of the Church? For reasons which we have no time to explain here, we think that a separate schema on the missions should be drafted. But there should at least be a much clearer explanation here of the dogmatic basis of missions.

For what do we see, Venerable Fathers? We see that in practice—and I speak here not only of those Churches which have been established for centuries—despite the admiration which everyone professes for missions to the pagans, there exists at the same time a practical indifference toward them as though missions were something extra, to be left to a few idealists.

We see another danger. Twenty years ago a book by two priests, Godin and Daniel, *France, a Mission Country,* stirred up many people, and a few years ago a famous cardinal reminded us that the Church is "in a state of mission", which means that everyone who is baptized has the duty of winning his brothers to Christ. Do we exaggerate when we suggest that these books were influential in evoking that pastoral concern which was so evident in the first session of this Council? But to us, bishops working in non-Christian lands, it seems that the way the word "missions" is now used in Europe is not free of ambiguity and danger. There is *ambiguity:* for the same word is used to designate a more realistic and active pastoral approach in regions where, despite the disease of neo-paganism, Christianity has long since sunk deep roots, and is also applied to the preaching of the Gospel among those peoples which have never been Christian, indeed know nothing of Christ. There is *danger:* for in this way the concept of mission can lose its power of stimulation and the "missionary spirit" which impels us to cry out "Woe to me if I do not preach the Gospel" can be destroyed. Will there not then be those among us, indeed, are there not those already who think they have fulfilled their missionary obligation if they establish an active pastoral program in their own diocese?

Let us not forget that the words, "Go and make all nations my disciples" were addressed to the *whole apostolic College.* Therefore every bishop, no matter who he is, shares this solemn responsibility of the Church, and should work according to his strength to expand the mission to the pagans.

But what do we see, Venerable Brothers? If statistics are compiled of all the apostolic work which is done for the good of souls by priests and religious in the whole world, would not this be the result? By far the greatest part of the work— even in many of the territories of Propaganda Fide —is taken up with a pastoral program of conservation (I do not use the word pejoratively), that is, in preserving the faith and morals of Catholics, in other words, of the "just" who are hardly in need of repentance. Considerably less apostolic work is devoted to bringing back to the Church those who have fallen away from her through loss of faith or moral lapses, in other words, to the sheep who have been lost of the house of Israel. But when we come to the immense mass of unbelievers, more than two billion pagans, they hardly receive the crumbs that fall from the table.

Hardly 5%, perhaps not even 3% of the apostolic labors of the Church are devoted to them.

For one who reflects in Christ Jesus, is not this a deplorable, indeed an intolerable situation?

It is easy for bishops and religious superiors in areas we call "traditionally Christian" to think, even though they have hundreds, even thousands of priests and members, that they cannot do more without depriving their dioceses or the works of their order of the necessary support. But what do they mean by "necessary"? Does it not sometimes mean "what has usually been done" or what is based on a static concept of Church organization? Are there not many pastors of small parishes, many professors, many religious preachers or confessors who have a number of free hours after they have satisfactorily accomplished their regular work? And are there not many priests and religious tied up in work that laymen could do just as well? Could we not send many subjects to strictly missionary tasks if we put through a bold program of reorganization? No matter how useful and praiseworthy the ministry they exercise at home, let us not forget that to spread the kingdom of God and of his Christ is even more laudable and precious.

The concrete form in which this cooperation of bishops could be organized can be dealt with elsewhere.

There is one thing we want to say: The missionary task of the Church in the strict sense should be more sharply stated and given a longer theological explanation in this place where its mystery is discussed. Otherwise we will have no hope for a kind of "Copernican revolution" in the Church, which consists in all the bishops of the world treating the needs of the missionary Church as true needs of their own diocese.

Archbishop of Bombay,
India

9

Not Domination
but Service

... There are also certain aspects of the Church missing or not adequately dealt with, as some of the speakers have already pointed out.

Since time is short (time wings away and never returns) allow me to point out one of these aspects which seems very important if we are to clear away a false image of the Church common among outsiders. Here in the Council we are taking into consideration conditions in both the West and the East. In those areas where Christians are the majority the Church is accused of wanting to rule the State. In non-Christian regions the Church is often treated as a State within a State. I do not mean to suggest, much less affirm, that this is the fault of the Church, but frequently it is the fault of Christians, especially those who want to be "more Catholic than the Pope". False concepts do not derive only from the bad will of one side, but often from a lack of wisdom and prudence on the other.

To clear away such prejudices, we must show the true face of the Church, so that all ambition to dominate is removed from it. Now in all this first chapter, the Church seems to be an end in itself, the terminus of the redemption, and not a community *open to the world* whose role is not to dominate but to *minister* and *serve*.

The idea of ministering is mentioned, but in relation to Christ and his Mystical Body, *not in relation to the world*. We know well that the sacrifice of the Mass and the sacraments manifest the idea of service. The *Sacrifice of the Mass,* for instance, is that sacramental action in which Jesus Christ gave his life for us. The *Sacrament of Baptism* is the Christian call to the service of Christ and his Church. The *Sacrament of Confirmation* is the call to take up the burden and privilege of adulthood, and so forth for all the sacraments and sacramentals. But true though it is that the Church exists *in herself,* she does not exist *for herself.* That is to say, the Church does not exist to dominate the world, but to serve the world; not to get privileges from the world but to suffer for the world. The Church is a minority, a powerful, bold and fervent minority—at the service of the majority. The distinguished Cardinal Newman, whom John XXIII mentions in his encyclical *Ad Petri Cathedram,* explained this idea very well in these words: "Grow we must, it is a prerogative of our apostolic origin. But of what value is growth in numbers without a corresponding moral manifestation of the community?" Newman, as his letters show, did not believe in what today we call "mass conversion", but in the con-

version of single individuals, so that each convert
might be a means of good Catholic formation;
an instrument of good for others.

I would like to remind you of the words the
Holy Father used on Sunday: "The world should
know that the Church constantly looks at her,
sincerely admires her and sincerely intends not to
dominate but serve, not to despise her but to increase her dignity, not to condemn her, but to
bring her comfort and salvation."

Is not the idea of service the constant teaching
of Christ? "That is not the way with you; among
you, whoever wants to be great must be your servant, and whoever wants to be first must be the
willing slave of all. For even the son of man did
not come to be served but to serve, and to surrender his life as a ransom for many" (Mark
10:43-45). "They were silent, because on the
way they had been discussing who was the greatest. He sat down, called the twelve, and said to
them: 'If anyone wants to be first, he must make
himself last of all and servant of all'" (Mark
9:33-34). And read also the twenty-fifth chapter
of Matthew on the last judgment. Now all this
holds not only for individual disciples, but also
for the whole Church. It is true that the Church
has been given kingly power. But this power is
spiritual and is practiced not by dominating
through force, but by effectively serving. Is not
the testimony of St. Paul the same. Let us read
Ephesians: "And these were his gifts: some to be
apostles, some prophets, some evangelists, some
pastors and teachers, to equip God's people for
work in his service, to the building of the body of

Christ" (4:11-12). And First Corinthians: "There are varieties of service, but the same Lord, there are many forms of work, but all of them, in all men, are the work of the same God" (12:4-6).

Since I speak as a bishop of India, let me add that these qualities are closely bound up with the missionary aim of the Church. We should be spurred on by the dynamism or missionary character of the Church: by her very nature the Church must grow and expand. But it must be crystal clear for the peoples to whom missionaries come that the Church does not want to expand in order, through increased numbers, to increase her power, but rather in order to serve the world and the truth more efficaciously and bear witness to Christ crucified and risen from the dead. "I have not come to be served, but to serve."

May I conclude my remarks by asking that this aspect of the face of the Church be brought out more clearly.

Someone may ask what will be, or what should be, the countenance or vision of the Church, suited to the modern mind, which this Synod wants to show to the world.

Will it be the image of a Church always on the alert to smoke out errors and heresy so she can condemn them? Will it be the image described by G. K. Chesterton, the English apologist: "The divine chariot flies thundering through the ages; the dull heresies sprawling and prostrate"? Will it be the image of the Church as Mother and Teacher?

Will it be the image of the Church in whose

bosom all peoples of the East and the West find a warm refuge and shelter?

Or will it be the image of the Church which is a "Servant Church" like her Founder, whose vicar on earth today wants to be called "the Servant of the Servants of God"?

Let those who are responsible decide.